JAMES BALDWIN

Douglas Field

First published in 2011 by Northcote House Publishers Ltd, Horndon, Tavistock, Devon, PL19 9NQ, United Kingdom.
Tel: +44 (01822) 810066. Fax: +44 (01822) 810034.

British Library Cataloguing-in-Publication Data
A catalogue record for this book is available from the British Library

ISBN 978-0-7463-1207-0 paperback

Typeset by TW Typesetting, Plymouth, Devon
Printed and bound in the United Kingdom

WRITERS AND THEIR WORK

ISOBEL ARMSTRONG
General Editor

the

JAMES BALDWIN

For my parents

Contents

Acknowledgements

I would like to thank the British Academy for awarding me a Small Research Grant, which enabled me to make several research trips to the United States. James Campbell kindly answered several questions with typical generosity. Thank you also to Eileen Ahearn and the James Baldwin estate for allowing me to quote from Baldwin's work. I am indebted to Emily Lordi for reading through the manuscript and offering many insightful suggestions. Thank you to Sarah Marie Leal for her support. Finally, a big thank you to Wayne, Jane and Hayley at North Tea Power for their friendship, hospitality and beautiful coffee.

Biographical Outline

1924   James Arthur Jones is born (2 August) in Harlem Hospital, New York City to Emma Berdis Jones. He does not know the identity of his biological father. Emma Berdis Jones marries David Baldwin and she and James take the name Baldwin.

1929   Attends Public School 24 in Harlem.

1935   Graduates from Public School 24 and enters Frederick Douglass Junior High School in Harlem where he is taught by Countee Cullen.

1938–42 Graduates from Frederick Douglass Junior High School and enters DeWitt Clinton High School in the Bronx.

1938–41 Writes for school magazine, *The Magpie*, and preaches at the Fireside Pentecostal Assembly.

1940   Meets the painter Beauford Delaney who becomes his mentor.

1942   Awarded high school diploma. Works as labourer at army depot in Belle Mead, New Jersey; is refused a hamburger for being 'colored' at restaurant in Princeton.

1943   David Baldwin, Sr dies (29 July); Baldwin meets Eugene Worth, a close friend who commits suicide in 1946.

1943–4 Lives and works in Greenwich Village.

1944   Meets Marlon Brando and Richard Wright.

1945   Starts literary magazine with Brad and Claire Burch, *This Generation*; awarded Eugene F. Saxton Foundation Fellowship after Wright's recommendation.

1947   Publishes reviews in *The Nation* and *The New Leader*.

1948	Awarded Rosenwald Fellowship and publishes with *Commentary*.
1948	Sails for Europe (11 November). Meets Themistocles Hoetis and Asa Benveniste, friends of Richard Wright and editors of the literary magazine, *Zero*.
1949	Publishes 'Everybody's Protest Novel' in the first edition of *Zero* (the essay was later published in *Partisan Review* in June); publishes 'Preservation of Innocence' in the second issue of *Zero*.
1948–57	Lives in Paris and the south of France and Switzerland.
1949	Sets off to Tangiers but falls ill and stays in Aix. Arrested for receiving stolen goods (December) and spends two weeks in Fresnes prison. Meets Lucien Happersberger a few days later.
1950	'The Death of a Prophet', a short story and draft of *Go Tell it on the Mountain* is published in *Commentary*.
1951–2	Spends winter with Happersberger in Loèche-les-Bains, Switzerland where he finishes *Go Tell it on the Mountain*.
1952	Meets Bernard Hasell, a dancer who becomes a life-long friend; borrows money from Marlon Brando to return to New York to publish his first novel; meets Ralph Ellison.
1953	*Go Tell it on the Mountain*; Beauford Delaney arrives in Paris.
1954	Returns to New York (June) and is awarded a fellowship at the MacDowell colony, New Hampshire (August).
1955	*Notes of a Native Son*; *The Amen Corner* is performed at Howard University and is attended by Sterling Brown and Alain Locke; Baldwin returns to Paris in October.
1956	*Giovanni's Room*; Baldwin takes overdose of sleeping pills; covers the Congrès des Ecrivains et Artistes Noirs (Congress of Negro Writers and Artists) for *Preuves* and *Encounter*.
1957	'Sonny's Blues' is published in *Partisan Review*; Baldwin returns to the United States. Visits the South for the first time in the autumn; meets Martin Luther King, Jr in Atlanta.

1958   The Actors Studio performs a workshop production of *Giovanni's Room* with Engin Cezzar in the title role. Baldwin returns to Paris.

1959   Travels to Sweden to interview film director Ingmar Bergman (October); meets Jean Genet in Paris.

1960   Visits the South (May) and becomes directly involved in the Congress of Racial Equality (CORE); interviews Martin Luther King, Jr; Richard Wright dies.

1961   *Nobody Knows My Name: More Notes of a Native Son*; Baldwin stays at William Styron's guest house in Connecticut where he works on *Another Country* and Styron writes *The Confessions of Nat Turner* (1967); meets the Honourable Elijah Muhammad; stays with Engin Cezzar in Turkey and meets David Leeming, one of his future biographers.

1961–9 Baldwin stays intermittently in Turkey and spends long periods from the end of 1964–7.

1962   *Another Country*; Baldwin travels to Senegal, Ghana and Sierra Leone with his sister Gloria.

1963   *The Fire Next Time*; Baldwin meets with US Attorney General Robert Kennedy (24 May); participates in the March on Washington (28 August); undertakes lecture tour for CORE.

1964   *Blues for Mister Charlie* opens at the ANTA Theater on Broadway (April 23, closing on August 29); Baldwin's name is added to the Security Index by the FBI and he complains to the Bureau about harassment. *Nothing Personal* (with Richard Avedon).

1965   *Going to Meet the Man*; Baldwin meets Bertrand Russell in London to discuss American action in Vietnam.

1967   Meets the Black Panther leadership in San Francisco after Huey Newton's arrest for the murder of a policeman; talks to Bobby Seale, the Chairman, and Eldridge Cleaver, Minister of Information.

1968   *Tell Me How Long the Train's Been Gone*; Baldwin works in Hollywood on a screenplay of *The Autobiography of Malcolm X* for Columbia Pictures; hosts a birthday party/fund-raising rally for Huey Newton in Oakland.

1969   *Baldwin's Nigger*, a documentary featuring Baldwin, directed by Horace Ové.

1971   *A Rap on Race* (with Margaret Mead); Baldwin moves to St Paul de Vence, near Nice, France where he is based until his death.

1972   *No Name in the Street, One Day When I Was Lost: A Scenario Based on the Autobiography of Malcolm X.*

1973   *A Dialogue* (with Nikki Giovanni).

1974   *If Beale Street Could Talk*. Baldwin is awarded centennial medal for 'the artist as prophet' from the Cathedral of St John the Divine, New York.

1976   *The Devil Finds Work, Little Man, Little Man: A Story of Childhood*.

1978   Teaches at Bowling Green University (and again in the autumn of 1979 and 1981).

1979   *Just Above My Head*; teaches at the University of California, Berkeley.

1980   Participates in the meeting of the African Literature Association in Gainesville, Florida with the Nigerian writer Chinua Achebe.

1981   Travels to Atlanta to write an article on the child murders that had occurred since 1979. The article becomes *The Evidence of Things Not Seen*.

1982   *I Heard it Through the Grapevine*, a documentary by Dick Fontaine about Baldwin revisiting the US South.

1983   *Jimmy's Blues: Selected Poems* (American edition published in 1985); musical version of *The Amen Corner* runs for six weeks at Ford's Theatre, Washington.

1983–6 Teaches five semesters at the University of Massachusetts.

1984   *Notes of a Native Son* is reprinted with a new introduction; Baldwin is hospitalized in Boston for heart problems.

1985   *The Evidence of Things Not Seen*; *The Price of the Ticket: Collected Non-Fiction, 1948–1985*; film version of *Go Tell it on the Mountain* airs on the Public Broadcasting System.

1986   Presented with French Legion of Honour by President Mitterrand; publishes his last article, 'To Crush the Serpent' in *Playboy*; *The Amen Corner* opens in London and is well received.

1987   Dies of cancer in St Paul de Vence, France (1 December); funeral is held at New York's Cathedral of St John the Divine (8 December); buried at Ferncliff Cemetery in Hartsdale, New York.

1989   Documentary directed by Karen Thorsen, *James Baldwin: The Price of the Ticket*; *Gypsies and Other Poems* (limited to 325 copies).

1998   Library of America publishes *James Baldwin: Collected Essays*, edited by Toni Morrison and *Early Novels and Short Stories*.

1999   Berdis Baldwin dies aged ninety-nine.

2004   James Baldwin stamp issued by US Postal Service.

Abbreviations

AC	*Another Country* [1962] (London: Penguin, 1990)
AD	*A Dialogue*, with Nikki Giovanni; foreword by Ida Lewis. Afterword by Orde Coombs (London: Michael Joseph, 1973)
BFMC	*Blues For Mister Charlie* [1965] (New York: Vintage, 1995)
CE	*James Baldwin: Collected Essays*, ed. Toni Morrison (New York: Library of America 1998)
CWJB	*Conversations with James Baldwin*, eds. Fred Standley and Louis H. Pratt (Jackson: University Press of Mississippi, 1989)
GR	*Giovanni's Room* [1956] (London: Penguin, 1990)
GTM	*Go Tell it on the Mountain* [1953] (London: Penguin, 1991)
GTMTM	*Going to Meet the Man* [1965] (London: Penguin, 1991)
IBSCT	*If Beale Street Could Talk* (London: Penguin, 1974)
JAMH	*Just Above My Head* [1979] (London: Penguin, 1994)
PT	*The Price of the Ticket: Collected Non-fiction, 1948–1985* (New York: St. Martin's/Marek, 1985)
TAC	*The Amen Corner* [1968] (London: Penguin, 1991)
TMHL	*Tell Me How Long the Train's Been Gone* [1968] (London: Penguin, 1994)

xvii

Introduction: Situating James Baldwin

Few twentieth century American authors have vexed, enraged or enthralled their readers as much as James Arthur Baldwin. At the height of his fame in the mid-1960s, Baldwin was one of the most photographed and frequently sought after American writers, speaking on prime-time television shows, writing for high-profile magazines and newspapers and appearing on the cover of *Time* magazine. His fiery and eloquent best-selling books, in particular his third novel *Another Country* (1962) and his essay *The Fire Next Time* (1963), transformed the landscape of American racial politics as he jabbed at his white liberal readers and cajoled the American nation. Although Baldwin is best known for being, in his words, 'a disturber of the peace', his vast body of work is far-reaching in terms of theme, content and genre (*CWJB* 171). Written over four tumultuous decades, Baldwin's *oeuvre* includes six novels, a number of book-length essays, plays, poetry, and book reviews, as well as a children's book and a scenario based on the life of Malcolm X. Baldwin was prodigious and prolific; his work reflects a fast-changing post-war political and cultural landscape, but he also helped to shape that landscape through his penetrating examinations of racial injustice, love, music and religion.

THE LIFE AND TIMES OF JAMES ARTHUR BALDWIN

In his work Baldwin repeatedly examines what he would call 'the price of the ticket', the price that white and black

Americans pay for accepting the myths of American history. His writing shines a torch into the labyrinthine structures of racial, sexual and class identities in post-war North America. Baldwin's own extraordinary journey began in Harlem in 1924 and ended in 1987 thousands of miles away in the south of France. During those sixty-three years, Baldwin moved from Harlem to Greenwich Village and from Paris to the American South; he stayed in Turkey and the United Kingdom and travelled to numerous countries across the globe. Baldwin's journey from impoverished Harlemite to a writer of international repute has been well documented by a handful of available biographies. Here, rather than re-treading old terrain, I will focus on a cluster of people that deeply influenced the author's life and work before he became an established writer.[1] I'll also give an overview of his literary output and then will consider his critical reputation before outlining the chapters of this book.

No other figure looms larger in Baldwin's early work than the man whom he called his father, David Baldwin. Jimmy, as he was known, was in fact born James Jones in 1924 and took the surname Baldwin when his mother, Emma Berdis, married David, a part-time preacher and labourer from New Orleans. Baldwin never knew the identity of his biological father and works such as his first novel, *Go Tell it on the Mountain* (1953) are shot through with references to illegitimacy. Much of Baldwin's work is preoccupied with finding – or creating – a place in the world. Working-class, African American, attracted both to men and women, Baldwin was, he later wrote, 'a kind of bastard of the West' (*CE* 7). His early work – and in particular his first novel and essay collection – invokes, recalls and at times rails against David Baldwin, 'the most bitter man I have ever met' (*CE* 64). 'I had not known my father very well', Baldwin recalled. 'We had got on badly' (*CE* 63).

David Baldwin's bitterness may have stemmed, his son suggests, from his inability to feed a quickly expanding family. As a young child Baldwin grew up during the 'Jazz Age', an era made famous by the Harlem Renaissance. For the Baldwins however, the aesthetic and political advancements of the black literati had little impact on their lives. As Baldwin recalled, the

2

notion of 'racial uplift' meant little to men such as his father who 'knew that he was black but did not know that he was beautiful' (*CE* 64). Baldwin's childhood was characterized rather by the grinding poverty of post-Depression America where his father struggled to find work in a fickle labour market.

Unimpressed by his son's burgeoning academic flair, David Baldwin encouraged his son to read the Bible and to eschew worldly pleasures such as jazz music and films. In a poignant description, Baldwin describes his father 'sitting at the window, locked up in his terrors; hating and fearing every living soul including his children who had betrayed him, too, by reaching towards the world which had despised him' (*CE* 66). Between the ages of fourteen and seventeen, Baldwin capitulated and became a child preacher, although in a Pentecostal church, not a Baptist church like his father. Baldwin's three years as a 'holly roller' preacher left an indelible mark on his writing and outlook which I explore in the final chapter of this book. When, aged seventeen, his father asked 'You'd rather write than preach, wouldn't you?' Baldwin answered, 'Yes', recalling that this was 'the one time in all our life together when we had really spoken to each other' (*CE* 80, 79).

In an interview about his first novel, *Go Tell it on the Mountain*, Baldwin recalled that he had to 'understand the forces, the experience, the life that shaped him [his father] before I could grow up myself, before I could become a writer' (*CWJB* 161). Baldwin attempted to lay his past to rest with an earlier draft of the novel titled 'Crying Holy', followed by three thematically similar short stories that are characterized by painful father-son relationships: 'In My Father's House', 'The Death of a Prophet', and 'Roy's Wound'. His first novel, Baldwin recalled, 'took me to ten years to write', adding that he 'became a writer by tearing up that book for ten years' (*CWJB* 161). The book in a sense marks Baldwin's attempts to understand his father: to articulate the terrors that stifled this embittered man. 'There was something in him', Baldwin wrote in 'Notes of a Native Son', 'groping and tentative, which was never expressed and which was buried with him' (*CE* 65).

Baldwin's uneasy relationship with his father could not be more different from his long friendship with the painter Beauford Delaney, whom he met as a teenager. Delaney, by then nearing forty, was homosexual and the son of a preacher. He was the first successful black artist that Baldwin had met; and for nearly four decades he would be Baldwin's 'spiritual father'.[2] Delaney introduced the teenage Baldwin to blues and jazz, allowing the young protégé to understand that these 'secular' sounds were as sacred as the music heard in church. In a remarkable recollection of their early encounters, Baldwin explains how Delaney's discussions of light and sound enabled Baldwin 'to begin to see', and also to hear – not just listen.[3] In Delaney's apartment Baldwin experienced an aural epiphany: 'I began to hear what I had never dared or been able to hear. Beauford never gave me any lectures. But . . . I really began to *hear* Ella Fitzgerald, Ma Rainey, Louis Armstrong, Bessie Smith . . .' (*PT* x).

If Delaney opened Baldwin's eyes and ears to other worlds around him, Richard Wright, the celebrated African American writer, gave him important and early support. When the young Baldwin knocked on Wright's door in Brooklyn in the early 1940s, he was welcomed by the Mississippian who saw promise in the draft of his first novel. Though *Go Tell it on the Mountain* would not be published for nearly ten years, Wright saw enough potential in the manuscript to recommend the young writer for a Eugene F. Saxon Fellowship of $500. When Wright left America for Paris in 1947, Baldwin was not far behind. He left for the French capital with barely forty dollars in his pocket in 1948.

Baldwin may well have been in awe of Wright when they first met in New York and no doubt first knocked on his door with some trepidation. The author of *Native Son* (1940) was the most famous living black American writer. After a year in Paris, however, Baldwin would write his first major essay, 'Everybody's Protest Novel', an essay which questioned the very fabric of Wright's literary and political reputation. Baldwin declared that protest fiction, of which he framed Wright as the most famous living proponent, could not deal with the complexity of modern life. Such an approach, Baldwin argued, was not only outdated but simplistic. These charges would ironically haunt Baldwin himself during the late 1960s as younger black radicals such as Eldridge Cleaver savaged his literary and political reputation.

Although Baldwin's early years seem to be marked by father-son relationships, he was a gregarious and sociable young man who forged a number of long-lasting friendships in his early years, including school friends Emile Capouya and Richard Avedon, both of whom became successful in later life: Capouya as literary editor of the *The Nation* and Avedon as a famous photographer and collaborator with Baldwin on the book *Nothing Personal* (1964). Less well known is Baldwin's friendship with Eugene Worth, a young African American whom Baldwin met in the early 1940s. In the introduction to *The Price of the Ticket*, Baldwin recalls that Worth, a man 'I loved with all my heart', committed suicide by hurling himself off George Washington Bridge in 1946 (*PT* xii), as does Rufus Scott, the protagonist of his third novel, *Another Country*. Worth appears only twice in Baldwin's essays: in the introduction to *The Price* and in a 1961 essay 'The New Lost Generation', and yet Worth's death and friendship impacted significantly on the budding writer. Firstly, Baldwin credits Worth with his brief involvement in Leftist political circles, where the aspiring writer became a member of the Young People's Socialist League and started his career writing for magazines associated with the New York Intellectuals, including *The Nation*, *Commentary* and *New Leader* (*PT* xii). Though he and Worth were not lovers, Baldwin would later write, 'I think I wish we had been', a parenthetical reminder of the young author's search for love at a time when it was dangerous to be black, difficult to be openly homosexual and perilous to be both (*PT* xii). Worth, Baldwin states clearly, 'would not have died in such a way and certainly not so soon, if he had not been black' (*CE* 661). Fearing that he would suffer a similar fate, Baldwin resolved to leave America.

FROM *GO TELL IT ON THE MOUNTAIN* TO *JUST ABOVE MY HEAD*

By 1951 Baldwin had established himself as a promising young writer but he had yet to publish a novel. That year he met the seventeen-year-old Lucien Happersberger, who invited the writer to finish *Go Tell it on the Mountain* in his native Swiss village of Loèche-les-Bains. Baldwin's painfully autobiographical novel is set in Harlem during the 1930s and the Swiss village was an incongruous but productive place to finish his first book, an experience he later wrote about in his 1953 essay 'Stranger in the Village'. With the help of another friend, Marlon Brando, Baldwin secured enough money to sail to New York where Knopf agreed to publish his first novel. Reviews were largely positive and critics singled out Baldwin's skilful employment of flashbacks and his sensitivity to the setting of the church, a theme he developed in his first play, *The Amen Corner* (performed in 1955 but not published until 1968).

Baldwin's second book, *Notes of a Native Son*, was published in 1955 and heralded the author as one of the most talented contemporary American essayists. Readers and critics were captivated by his unique blend of syncopated prose that drew on a range of influences from the King James Bible to Henry James. Part autobiography, part social and political commentary, Baldwin's essays included an achingly poignant account of his relationship with his father ('Notes of a Native Son'), his notorious essay 'Everybody's Protest Novel', and reflections on his experience as a black American in Paris. By the time his second collection of essays appeared in 1961 (*Nobody Knows My Name: More Notes of a Native Son*), Baldwin was on the brink of becoming a major American – not just African American – writer.

If readers of *Go Tell it* were expecting his second novel to build on the themes of African American community and culture then many would have been surprised and puzzled by *Giovanni's Room*, published in 1956. Set in Paris with no African American characters, Baldwin's novel tells the story of David, an American abroad, who falls in love with the eponymous Italian bartender, Giovanni. Baldwin's first commercial success, *Another Country* (1962), returned to the US through its setting in Manhattan and tackled a range of provocative themes including love, racism and loneliness. Despite poor reviews by contemporary New York critics, many of whom were unsettled by the descriptions of interracial and bisexual relationships, *Another Country* hit the best-seller lists.

Baldwin's controversial novel, which I explore later in this book, was followed by one of the most explosive and searing essays on civil rights in America. *The Fire Next Time* originally published in the *New Yorker*, was a much publicized bestseller. Written in Baldwin's inimitable blend of coruscating prose that is both personal and political, *The Fire Next Time* called upon America to acknowledge that the 'black problem' in the United States was in fact a white one. By 1963 Baldwin was seen as a major voice of black America. He appeared on the cover of *Time* magazine in 1963, where according to the article within, 'today there is not another writer – white or black – who expresses with such poignancy and abrasiveness the dark realities of the racial ferment in North and South'.[4] Baldwin continued to expose the ugly realities of racial injustice in his play *Blues for Mister Charlie* (1964). Set in the American South in the early 1960s and loosely based on the murder of Emmett Till (a teenager lynched for whistling at a white girl), Baldwin's play, according to LeRoi Jones (now Amiri Baraka) 'announced the Black Arts Movement'.[5]

Baldwin's next three major works continued to focus on civil rights and black radical politics – although not always in expected ways. His collection of short stories *Going to Meet the Man* (1965), written over a number of years, ranges from echoes of *Go Tell it on the Mountain* ('The Rockpile' and 'The Outing') to the title story told through the eyes of a white sheriff. 'Going to Meet the Man', the tale of a racist sheriff who harbours a secret desire for black women, also highlights Baldwin's preoccupations with the psychosexual landscape of America, where sexual desire and racism are inextricably intertwined. The collection also contains Baldwin's most widely anthologized story, 'Sonny's Blues', which explores the themes of alienation, community and music through the tale of two estranged brothers.

Baldwin's last novel of the 1960s, *Tell Me How Long the Train's Been Gone* (1968), explores the role of an aging actor who struggles, like the author, to reconcile the twin roles of artist and spokesman, a theme he would return to with a mixture of candour and circumspection in his long essay, *No Name in the Street* (1972). In 1974 Baldwin published his penultimate novel, *If Beale Street Could Talk*, a meditation on the inequities of the American judicial system, narrated by a pregnant black woman. Baldwin continued to flout narrative and generic convention with his next major work, *The Devil*

Finds Work (1976), a largely misunderstood blend of memoir and film criticism. As with *Nothing Personal*, his 1964 photo-text collaboration with Richard Avedon, Baldwin's work on visual media has been largely ignored by critics. His last novel, *Just Above My Head* (1979), a long and wide-ranging tale of gospel singers and civil rights activism, is generally acknowledged as his last major book. His poetry collection, *Jimmy's Blues* (1983) has been forgotten by critics and Baldwin struggled to find a publisher for *The Evidence of Things Not Seen* (1985), a long essay on child murders in Atlanta. In 1985, however, Baldwin's reputation was revived by the publication of *The Price of the Ticket*, a volume that collects his selected non-fiction from 1948–1985.

CRITICAL REPUTATION

In recent years there has been a renewed interest in Baldwin's life and work, which I trace in the conclusion. In 1998 the Library of America published two volumes of his work edited by Toni Morrison and in 2004 the US Postal Office issued a James Baldwin stamp. Despite these acts of canonization, Baldwin's literary reputation is far from secure. In contrast to the steadfast reputations of Richard Wright or Ralph Ellison (African American writers to whom he is often compared), Baldwin is often seen as a talented maverick who never quite fulfilled his early promise. Many readers and critics see his first novel, *Go Tell it on the Mountain*, as his most technically accomplished work. The critical consensus suggests that Baldwin's craft declined after (and perhaps mid-way through) *Another Country*. Most critics claim that Baldwin was an exceptional essayist whose non-fiction roared and soared as his fiction spiralled out of narrative control. (His later fiction, as I discuss in the following chapters, is woefully neglected.) Baldwin is remembered for his contributions to the Civil Rights movement (*The Fire Next Time*) and for his widely anthologized short story 'Sonny's Blues', but his wider work is largely overlooked for reasons that I'll explore.

In a particularly revealing interview in the 1970s, Baldwin referred to himself as 'all those strangers called Jimmy Baldwin'

(*CWJB* 79). He was, as he knew only too well, many things to many people. Or, as he wrote in *No Name in the Street*, 'what in the world was I by now but an aging, lonely, sexually dubious, politically outrageous, unspeakably erratic freak?' (*CE* 363). Baldwin represents a particular challenge to literary critics who are often unsettled by writers who revel in contradictions. America, Baldwin wrote early in his career, is a 'country devoted to the death of the paradox' (*CE* 17). As I explore in this book his work repeatedly challenged the very limitations and definitions that much scholarship has stubbornly refused to give up. Over the years, Baldwin's reputation has suffered from critics who insist he must be black *or* gay, religious *or* secular; that his legacy lies in the essay, not the novel; that his work suffered from his twin roles as spokesman and artist.

This book is structured around key themes in Baldwin's life and work, areas which necessarily cross over from one chapter to another. By organizing the chapters thematically I am not attempting to straight jacket Baldwin's work but rather to show how his writing crosses over from one theme to the next, much like the itinerant writer himself. The chapters, in other words, are also reminders that his work cannot be contained in one or other border. While I have tried to do justice to the range of Baldwin's work, I have necessarily had to select works from his *oeuvre*. Chapter 1, 'Transnational Baldwin', maps out the writer's literal journeys from Harlem to Greenwich Village, from New York to Paris. Here I consider Baldwin as an expatriate writer whose major works were published outside of the United States. I examine Baldwin's meditations on what it means to be American and also explore the impact of his self-imposed exile. I consider how exile equipped Baldwin with a critical distance that refracted and distilled his insightful analyses of post-war America.

Despite his repeated claims that he was an artist, not a spokesman, Baldwin became the most prominent writer to chronicle and critique the US Civil Rights movement, which I examine in Chapter 2, 'The Writer and the Civil Rights Movement'. Unlike Richard Wright, who died in 1960, or Ralph Ellison, who believed that political activism diluted the artist's talent, Baldwin's career is characterized by his commitment to, and preoccupation with, the civil rights movement. Baldwin made a number of trips to the American South in the 1950s and produced some of the most incendiary and penetrating commentaries on racial injustice, most famously in his long essays *The Fire Next Time* and later *No Name in the Street*.

Although Baldwin was a visible and vocal civil rights activist, public perception of his homosexuality complicated his reputation as an authoritative voice on racial politics, a phenomenon I discuss in Chapter 3, 'Racial and Sexual Difference'. In recent years, Baldwin has emerged as a key progenitor of queer black studies and yet his own writing and interviews reveal a complicated relationship to any one identifiable sexual category or movement. In contrast to his pioneering treatments of homosexuality and bisexuality in his fiction, only three of his published essays overtly discuss homosexuality. I trace the ways in which Baldwin's writing complicates a straightforward reading of his sexual identities and explore the complex relationship between blackness and homosexuality. During the book I have, where possible, referred to Baldwin as 'queer' rather than homosexual. As I point out in Chapter 3, Baldwin had little truck with the limiting sexual categories of 'straight', 'homosexual' 'gay', or 'bisexual'. My use of the term 'queer' is intended to signal his writing about sexual practice that differs from the 'norm' of American heterosexuality, while trying to avoid aligning what we 'know' about Baldwin's sexual practice with readings of his work. Here I share Gary Holcomb's preference for the use of 'queer' in relation to the Jamaican writer Claude McKay. For Holcomb, 'Queer does not merely articulate a sexual orientation or preference or even a social identity or classification'. By using the term 'queer' my aim is not to diminish Baldwin's importance as a pioneering writer of bisexual and homosexual novels and essays, but to draw attention to the ways in which he 'repudiates the notion that sexuality is limited by social practices and classificatory systems, that the human subject is reducible to scientific and therefore ideological arrangements'.[6]

In Chapter 4, 'Baldwin and Music', I trace the writer's use of and writing about jazz, blues and gospel music through a reading of *Another Country*, the short story 'Sonny's Blues', and his final novel *Just Above My Head*. I consider how and why Baldwin's work is punctuated with references to music and how his engagement with music connects to his relationship with the church, the subject of Chapter 5. In the final chapter, 'Baldwin and Religion', I explore Baldwin's deep criticism of, yet persistent preoccupation with, the church. His work is testament to the power and importance of black religious experience but Baldwin remains one of the fiercest critics of the strictures of the church.

1

Transnational Baldwin

FROM NATIVE SON TO TRANSATLANTIC CELEBRITY

The issuance of the James Baldwin postal stamp in 2004 was not only a sign that the late author had (again) gained national recognition; it was also a fitting tribute to a writer who described himself as a 'transatlantic commuter' (*CWJB* 256). Baldwin's life began in Harlem Hospital in 1924 and ended sixty three years later in the south of France where he had made his home. Baldwin's journey along the way, both literal and metaphorical, was long, often hard and frequently unpredictable. The writer's travels took him from Harlem to Paris, to the American South and included trips to London and Senegal as well as an intermittent decade in Turkey. Travel was not just an interest for Baldwin but part of his life as a writer; he wrote in many places and moved through many genres. Baldwin lugged around his first novel, *Go Tell it on the Mountain* (1953) for ten years; he began writing the novel in New York, took it to Paris and finished it in Switzerland. His first major essay, 'Everybody's Protest Novel' (1949) was published in *Zero*, a small literary magazine edited by two Americans in Paris. His third novel, *Another Country* (1962), along with many other of his most important works, was finished in Istanbul. Baldwin ends his long essay, *No Name in the Street*, by noting that the book was written in New York, San Francisco, Hollywood, London, Istanbul and St Paul de Vence.

As the titles of so many of Baldwin's works attest – *Another Country*, 'Stranger in the Village', *Nobody Knows My Name* and *No Name in the Street* – his work is preoccupied with ideas of home and belonging. Baldwin's titles frequently invoke a sense of place or the elusiveness of place: *Go Tell it on the Mountain, Giovanni's Room* and *Just Above My Head*. It's important to remember, too, that most of Baldwin's work was published outside of North America even though few of his novels or short stories reflect his itinerant life style. France, for example, features prominently in only two of his fictional works (*Giovanni's Room* and the short story, 'This Morning, This Evening, So Soon', 1960). Puerto Rico is imagined briefly in *If Beale Street Could Talk* (1974) and Côte d'Ivoire in *Just Above My Head* (1979), but Turkey does not appear in any novel, despite his long association with Istanbul. As suggested by Baldwin's revealing comments in Sedat Pakay's 1970 film, *James Baldwin: From Another Place*, it was precisely his distance from North America that enabled him to write more acutely about his birthplace: 'One sees [one's country] better from a distance . . . from another place, another country'.[1]

Much of Baldwin's work is preoccupied with what it means to be American, his ideas and experiences forged in the crucible of exile which, his writing suggests, sharpened his perspectives on the fast-changing nation of his birth. As I explore below, exile was an important part of Baldwin's creative process: to remain in the United States, Baldwin suggested in his essay 'The Discovery of What it Means to be an American' (1959), was to view the world with cataracts, the artist's vision blurred by the proximity to the racial and social nightmare of the civil rights era. In what follows I map Baldwin's journeys from Harlem to the south of France, noting how the writer's views on exile and nationhood shifted, and paying attention to Baldwin's developing views on transnational black culture. By focusing on his main collections of essays, I want to chart his transition from native son to international writer, one who was increasingly concerned with North America's position in the global arena of imperialism, whether militarily, culturally or financially. As I argue in this chapter, Baldwin's essays in particular are incisive commentaries on what it means to be American in the midst of the Cold War, civil rights, Vietnam and the emergence of black radical politics. I also consider how his work fits into wider narratives about black transnational culture by considering his views on Africa and his observations about black Francophone writers in Paris.

13

THE EARLY YEARS: FROM NEW YORK INTELLECTUAL TO NATIVE SON

Baldwin's career as a writer began at school when he edited the DeWitt Clinton school paper between 1940 and 1942. DeWitt was an impressive school in the Bronx which fostered the young writer's talent. After graduating, Baldwin moved from Harlem to Greenwich Village where, through his friendship with Beauford Delaney, he landed a job working at the Calypso, a popular restaurant with artists and writers, including Claude McKay, Alain Locke and C. L. R. James. In 1945 Baldwin published work in a short-lived literary magazine, *The Generation*, edited by Brad Burch, a former school friend. By 1947 Baldwin started to write book reviews for several prominent left-wing magazines associated with the New York intellectuals, most notably *The Nation*, *The New Leader*, *Commentary* and later *Partisan Review*. Baldwin reviewed a wide variety of books including works on Catholic philosophy (*The Person and the Common Good*), Brooklyn Jewish gangs (*The Amboy Dukes*), and two works about Robert Louis Stevenson. In his first review of a book on African American literature, Shirley Graham's *There Was Once a Slave: The Heroic Story of Frederick Douglass* (1947), Baldwin is critical of the award-winning book by W. E. B. Du Bois's future wife. The review is notable for the ways in which it anticipates Baldwin's famous critique of Harriet Beecher Stowe's 1852 novel, *Uncle Tom's Cabin* in 'Everybody's Protest Novel'. Baldwin argues that Graham, has 'robbed him [Douglass] of dignity and humanity by glossing over any of the abolitionist's imperfections', foreshadowing his pronouncement that Uncle Tom 'has been robbed of his humanity' (*CE* 14).[2] Graham's portrait of Douglass, like Stowe's characterization of Uncle Tom, is little more than the flip-side of the 'tradition that Negroes are never to be characterized as anything than amoral, laughing clowns'.[3] Baldwin issues a call for greater complexity here that would become a characteristic of his fiction and non-fiction.

Baldwin's move to Paris in 1948, a year after Richard Wright had moved there, precipitated his transition from acerbic reviewer to accomplished and startling essayist. In 1949

Baldwin was invited to contribute an essay to *Zero*, a newly formed literary journal edited by two Americans, Albert 'Asa' Benveniste and Themistocles Hoetis (now known as George Solomos). Baldwin's first contribution was his seminal essay 'Everybody's Protest Novel', which picks apart Stowe's *Uncle Tom's Cabin* and ends with an unflinching critique of Richard Wright's landmark 1940 novel, *Native Son*. For Baldwin, Stowe's 'very bad novel', fails to raise consciousness about slavery beyond the thrill and sense of virtue that comes from reading the book (*CE* 11). 'The "protest" novel', Baldwin writes, 'so far from being disturbing, is an accepted and comforting aspect of the American scene, ramifying that framework we believe to be so necessary' (*CE* 15). In a brief but acerbic analysis of *Native Son*, Baldwin argues that Wright's protagonist, Bigger Thomas, is little more than the polar opposite of Uncle Tom. If Stowe characterized Tom as an emasculated, forbearing slave, Baldwin argued that Wright's Bigger Thomas becomes a caricature of the black killer and rapist. Wright's failure, Baldwin argues, is that Bigger 'has accepted a theology that denies him life', a theme that he extends to the genre of protest fiction (*CE* 18).

Much has been written about Baldwin's famous article, not least because it marked his entrance as a major new literary talent and did so by attacking the most famous African American writer of his time. Amidst the furore generated by Baldwin's essay, critics have overlooked its publication history. It was first published in *Zero* and not as often attributed, *Partisan Review*. His essay was soon republished in *Partisan Review* and later in *Perspectives USA*, an anti-Stalinist magazine started in the 1950s 'to woo European intellectuals to the side of freedom'.[4] In *Zero*, Baldwin's essay was published alongside poetry and stories by an impressive transnational cast of writers, including Christopher Isherwood and William Carlos Williams. In a strange twist, Richard Wright's story, 'The Man Who Killed a Shadow', was placed just before Baldwin's damning essay of the older writer, which could only have further strained relations between the two writers.

Baldwin's second essay in the following issue of *Zero*, 'Preservation of Innocence', was a bold discussion of homosexuality. In sharp contrast to 'Everybody's Protest Novel', this essay was not republished by *Partisan Review* and it was conspicuously absent from *The Price of the Ticket*, remaining uncollected until the 1998 Library of America volume. 'Preservation' is one of only three of Baldwin's published essays to discuss homosexuality openly. Baldwin may have been emboldened to publish this essay abroad but he did not discuss the themes of blackness and sexuality together in his early work. Though he would write a pioneering novel about homosexual love while living in Paris (*Giovanni's Room*), the main protagonist is white, suggesting, as Baldwin himself acknowledged, the difficulties of treating blackness and homosexuality (even while abroad) during the conservative cold war of the 1950s. Baldwin's two essays in *Zero* marked a turning point in the writer's career; from reviewer to essayist, from reviewer to a trans-Atlantic commentator. In 1950 *Commentary* published 'The Death of a Prophet', a fragmented draft of *Go Tell it* and one of the few stories in the journal that did not deal with a Jewish theme. In the same year, 'The Negro in Paris' was published in *Reporter* (the title would be changed to 'Encounter in the Seine: Black meets Brown'), followed by several now collected pieces, including a second article for *Partisan Review*, 'Many Thousands Gone' in 1951. Not long after Baldwin's first novel was published in 1953 he was starting to command well-paid fees for his articles, which appeared in *Harper's*, *Encounter*, *Mademoiselle*, and, by the end of the 1950s, *The New York Times Book Review*.

Although Baldwin's early essays in Paris announced his arrival as a promising and talented writer, his reputation in France began, Rosa Bobia notes, 'in slow motion', for a number of significant reasons, not least the late translation of *Go Tell it on the Mountain*, which was not published in France until 1957.[5] When Baldwin arrived in Paris, he was writing first under the shadow of Richard Wright, and then later Chester Himes, whose detective fiction was extremely popular in France. After Wright's death in 1960 – and in particular after the publication of *The Fire Next Time* in 1963 – Baldwin was increasingly seen as *the* voice of black America by the French reading public. In the 1950s, however, in sharp contrast to Wright, Baldwin seemed to avoid alliances with other intellectual communities, whether African American, black Francophone or other expatriate writers. In 'Equal in Paris' Baldwin recalled that during his early years in the French capital he 'floated, so to speak, on a sea of acquaintances', adding that he 'knew almost no one' (*CE* 103). As I explore, Baldwin's essays about Paris focus on the *lack* of community among African Americans and black Francophone writers and students, what he describes in 'Encounter on the Seine' as the black American's 'deliberate isolation' (*CE* 86). Baldwin's relationship with Wright, for example, was strained, if not tense, something that an FBI report picked up on in 1955. According to the report (which erroneously describes Baldwin as a student), Baldwin attacked Wright's Franco-American Fellowship Group, set up in 1951 to sponsor young writers. 'Wright and his group', the report states, 'were the target of attacks from one James Baldwin'.[6] Unlike Wright who was on the editorial board of *Présence Africaine* and actively involved in Sartre's Rassemblement Democratique Révolutionnaire, Baldwin kept his distance from established intellectual or artistic communities.[7]

Baldwin's relationship to exile is anything but straightforward but his views on what is now called transatlantic or transnational culture illustrate a number of key characteristics, particularly in what we might call his 'Paris Essays'; 'Encounter on the Seine' (1950), 'Equal in Paris' (1955) and 'Princes and Powers' (1957). As I will show through a reading of his important essay, 'The Discovery of What it Means to be an American', his views on exile and nationality developed. In his early essays, Baldwin was clearly sceptical about how black international artists could collaborate; his later work suggests the importance of transatlantic collaboration in the black diaspora. However, several key themes run through his early reflections and observations of what it meant to be an American in Paris. Firstly, Baldwin is quick to quash the romanticism of exile and in particular the myth of Paris as a city of carefree lovers. In 'A Question of Identity' he writes that Paris is, 'according to its legend, the city where everyone loses his head, and his morals, lives through at least one *histoire d'amour*', but this fiction, he writes, is 'unlivable', a fable from the past (*CE* 93). In reality, life for those in the American student colony in Paris is 'a private, and very largely speechless affair' (*CE* 91).

17

Baldwin's essays on Paris are punctuated with references to isolation and the difficulties of communication in ways that reveal much about his attitudes towards transnational exchange. In 'Encounter on the Seine', Baldwin observes that it is not only white and black Americans in Paris who share uneasy encounters, but there is little sense of community amongst expatriate African Americans. 'In general', Baldwin writes, 'only the Negro entertainers are able to maintain a useful and unquestioning comradeship with other Negroes' (*CE* 85). Baldwin suggests that black Americans who encounter one another in Paris may experience reminders of 'past humiliations' from the US to the extent that many African Americans live in 'deliberate isolation' (*CE* 86). Baldwin suggests that exile, far from connecting expatriates in fact creates isolation, troubling the critical romance of exile as engendering kinship and freedom – or at least drawing attention to the thin line between freedom and isolation.

If Baldwin stressed the collective 'unreadable face' of American expatriates in 'A Question of Identity', then his observations about the encounters between black Africans and African Americans in Paris amplify his views on the difficulties of cultural exchange through his numerous references to the difficulties of communication. In contrast to Wright who was a key player in conferences and committees that sought to foster political and artistic kinship with transnational black writers, Baldwin remained detached, even aloof from such projects. In 'Encounter', Baldwin is at pains to point out the cultural and linguistic differences that separate the African American from black students from the French colonies. 'They face each other, the Negro and the African', Baldwin writes, 'over a gulf of three hundred years – an alienation too vast to be conquered in an evening's good will, too heavy and too double-edged ever to be trapped in speech' (*CE* 89). Baldwin's claim that the African and African American, do not share a common language, are unable to communicate, anticipates his later comment that 'we almost needed a dictionary to talk'.[8]

'Encounter' is an insightful essay that distinguishes between the different forms of oppression experienced by black Americans and the colonial subjects he observes in Paris. Strangely, Baldwin's essay omits any discussion of the ways in which black Francophone students had made their own mark in artistic and intellectual collaborations which included African American writers. Alioune Diop's famous quarterly, *Présence Africaine*, was founded in 1947, the year before Baldwin arrived in Paris. It included contributions by African American writers such as Richard Wright and Gwendolyn Brooks. Baldwin not only neglects to mention Diop's journal but continues to stress the difficulties of communication and collaboration – whether socially or culturally – between black American artists and colonial writers of African descent.

Baldwin's cautious, even sceptical views on transnational interchange are illustrated by his essay 'Princes in Powers', his report of the first International Congress of Black Writers and Artists at the Sorbonne in Paris, 1956. The Congress, organized by Diop and others, was an historical gathering of artists and writers and international luminaries that included attendees from the Carribbeans, Africans, Francophones and African Americans. With the ambitious aim of discussing and establishing the international future and legacy of black political and artistic production, the Congress was a high profile event in Paris. In his role as reporter, rather than participant, Baldwin cast a critical eye over the proceedings, which included contributions from other black American artists such as Wright, Mercer Cook and John A. Davis. If the conference aimed at unifying people of African descent, Baldwin was quick to point out their inescapable differences. The Nigerian poet, M. Lasebikan, who speaks an 'extremely strange language', Baldwin writes, was 'dressed in a most arresting costume'; Baldwin adds that 'he was wearing a very subdued but very ornately figured silk robe, which looked Chinese, and he wore a red velvet toque, a sign, someone told me that he was a Mohammedan' (*CE* 148). Baldwin's description not only positions him as Western observer, but his rhetoric is reminiscent of colonial writing about Africa. Baldwin makes no attempt to understand Lasebikan's national dress, described here as a 'costume', and he erroneously identifies the poet's language as 'Youriba', rather than 'Yoruba' (*CE* 148). For Baldwin, rather than unifying the gathered artists of African descent, the conference in fact illustrated 'that gulf which yawns between the American Negro and all other men of color' (*CE* 146).

19

Baldwin's comments, though at times uncomfortable, in fact anticipate more recent theories on the complexity of the diaspora, illustrated by Brent Hayes Edwards's acclaimed book on 1920s and 1930s transnational black culture, *The Practice of the Diaspora: Literature, Translation and the Rise of Black Internationalism* (2003). Though Edwards maps out and draws attention to a significant number of black American works that engage with Europe, he stresses that 'the cultures of black internationalism can be seen only *in translation*'.[9] As Edwards points out, echoing Baldwin's reservations about cultural unity, such encounters between culturally and linguistically disparate people of African descent can enable alliances but also draw attention to differences. In 'Princes and Powers', Baldwin writes of a black transnational culture 'which has produced so many different subhistories, problems, traditions, possibilities, aspirations, assumptions, languages, hybrids', what Edwards calls 'unavoidable misapprehensions and misreadings, persistent blindness and solipsisms, self-defeating and abortive collaborations, a failure to translate even a basic grammar of blackness' (*CE* 152).[10]

In 'Princes and Powers' Baldwin repeatedly observes how identities are forged in specific historical conditions, a concept illustrated by his probing question, 'For what, beyond the fact that all black men at one time or another left Africa, or have remained there, do they really have in common?' (*CE* 152). At one point, Baldwin concedes that people of African descent *did* have something in common, though again he draws attention to the inexpressibility of this relationship. Baldwin muses on what he describes as black people's 'precarious . . . unutterably painful relation to the white world'. This was a comment that he would later redress (*CE* 153). In an interview eight years after the 1956 conference, he noted that he 'profoundly distrust[ed]' negritude, adding that 'oppressions do not necessarily unify so many millions of people all over the world':

> Well, how in the world is this going to connect to so many different experiences? To be born in Jamaica, Barbados, or Portugal, or New York, or to be black, wouldn't seem to me to be enough . . . and the situation of the man in Jamaica is not the situation of the man in Harlem at all.[11]

In 'Princes and Powers' Baldwin is careful to distinguish between the colonial experiences of Africans who wish to overthrow European white rule and the complicated relationship between black Americans and white authority in the US. He writes that 'It had never been in our interest to overthrow it'; rather, 'It had been necessary to make the machinery work for our benefit and the possibility of its doing so had been . . . built in' (*CE* 148). Baldwin here and elsewhere claims that African Americans do not have the option of revolution; they cannot destroy the 'house' of America, since they have nowhere else to go. As I discuss later in the book, Baldwin warned that the house was burning; at times he would suggest dousing the flames, and at others, tearing down the building brick by brick.

TRANSNATIONALITY IN BALDWIN'S FICTION

Baldwin's fiction is preoccupied with the transnationality of modern life where cities attract (or repel) hoards of migrants and exiles who are in search of money, love or salvation. Many of Baldwin's characters, like the author, are frequent travellers, in search of a sense of home. Life abroad enables Baldwin's characters to experience their sense of nationality, like Yves in *Another Country* who feels French for the first time as he arrives in New York or David in *Giovanni's Room* who is both annoyed at being called American but at a loss when not recognized as a US citizen (*AC* 424; *GR* 86). In Baldwin's fictional worlds, characters of different nationalities, often in cameo roles, rub shoulders with the American protagonists in ways that highlight the injustices of American life, also suggesting that national identity is a fiction. In *Giovanni's Room*, set in Paris, with forays in North America and the south of France, Baldwin's characters are an assembly of displaced figures. Giovanni has left his southern Italian village; as an economic migrant he stands in sharp contrast to the wealthy Belgian-born American businessman, Jacques. David, who has come to 'find himself' has never settled, growing up in Brooklyn, San Francisco, Seattle and New York. Although Paris gives David the illusion of freedom – 'with no-one to watch, no penalties attached' – the novel begins, as it ends, with David alone. For

David has 'run so far, so hard, across the ocean', only to find that he is once again confronted with himself (*GR* 11). In *Just Above My Head*, Julia travels to Africa, hoping to make sense of her life through an understanding of her heritage, an experience that remains unfulfilled as she is bowed down with cultural and linguistic obstacles. Baldwin is at pains to point out that travel can be a dangerous and isolated experience, illustrated by the image of Hall Montana, also in *Just Above My Head*, who dies alone in a London pub.

Baldwin does, however, suggest that exile and travel can have an enabling, even healing effect, a point that he suggests through the contrasting experience of two characters, both of whom are actors. In *Tell Me How Long the Train's Been Gone*, Leo Proudhammer, a black actor expresses a desire to travel away from his compatriots, whom he describes as 'the emptiest and most unattractive people in the world' (*TMHL* 282). Leo realizes that 'he would never be able to leave this country'; he is 'part of this people, no matter how bitterly I judged them' (*TMHL* 282). Although Leo is an actor, Baldwin suggests the connections between the typecast roles he is forced to play as an actor – 'porters, clowns and butlers' (*TMHL* 292) – and the ways in which he is treated by white Americans (*TMHL* 294). Here Leo voices Baldwin's concerns in his 1959 essay, 'The Discovery of What it Means to be an American', that if he remained in the US he would become '*merely* a Negro; or, even, merely a Negro writer' (*CE* 137).

If Baldwin suggests that Leo is stranded in the mire of racial expectation, then this is sharply contrasted by his portrayal of Eric, the white actor in *Another Country* who is first described in an Edenic garden in the south of France with his lover, Yves. Baldwin would later temper suggestions that his own life in France was a haven, stating 'I am *not* in exile and I am *not* in paradise. It rains down here, too', but the scene of bucolic sensuality in *Another Country* is staged as a refuge from the harsh metropolis of Manhattan (*CWJB* 154). Crucially, Eric and Yves are 'for the other, the dwelling place that each had despaired of finding' (*AC* 184), suggesting the ways in which 'other countries' in Baldwin's fiction are not only material countries, but interior landscapes of longing and belonging.

Eric functions as a catalyst or conduit for the main characters in *Another Country*: he sleeps with men and women, black and white, American and European, connecting Baldwin's cast of disparate characters. Importantly, Baldwin describes Eric's nationality as indeterminate: he 'did not look American, exactly; they [people in the bar] were wondering how to place him' (*AC* 245). Eric, unlike Leo (or Rufus in *Another Country*) occupies an enabling, albeit privileged, position. As an actor – and particularly as a white actor – Eric functions as Baldwin's ideal, one who cannot be placed – not just in terms of nationality – but in his sexuality and masculinity. Watching Eric on screen, Vivaldo observes that:

> It was the face . . . of a tormented man. Yet, in precisely the same way that great music depends, ultimately, on great silence, this masculinity was defined, and made powerful, by something which was not masculine. But it was not feminine either, and something in Vivaldo resisted the word *androgynous*. . . . But, as most women are not gentle, nor most men strong, it was a face which suggested, resonantly, in the depths, the truth about our natures.   (*AC* 324)

In Vivaldo's description Eric occupies the midway point between masculine and feminine, and in his bisexuality appears to be neither straight nor gay – just as he looks neither American nor French. And yet if Eric suggests an idealized identity that is unfettered by gender, sexuality or nationality, then Baldwin also suggests that this is a privilege founded on whiteness.

Some of Baldwin's most illuminating meditations on the themes of home, transnationalism and the slippery relationship between nationality and ethnicity can be found in two pieces that he wrote in the 1959 and 1960 respectively. In 'The Discovery of What it Means to be an American', first published in the *New York Times Book Review* (republished in *Nobody Knows My Name*), Baldwin begins with a quotation from Henry James: 'It is a complex fate to be an American' (*CE* 137). 'This Morning, This Evening, So Soon', the tale of an unnamed African American singer returning to the United States, explores the complexity of modern national identity, implicitly asking what it means to be American. The singer, loosely based on Harry Belafonte, has a Swedish wife and a son who has never been to the United States. He spends his last evening with his friend Vidal, a film director who was imprisoned in

Germany during the war and who has a daughter in England. As they drink in a bar they encounter Algerians and Tunisians and a group of young African American students in a discothèque that is frequented by Swedes, Greeks and Spaniards.[12]

In both his essay and short story, Baldwin suggests that exile – or at least living outside of America – is a necessary stage in the development of the artist: that the artist cannot truly create in the suffocating racial drama of 1950s America. The narrator of 'This Morning' concedes, both that he would not have met his Swedish wife in America, but also that he would probably have become a teacher or lawyer like his brother had he remained in the United States. Or, as Baldwin wrote in 'The Discovery', the American writer 'very often has to leave this country' in order to become an artist (*CE* 139). And yet despite Baldwin's more optimistic statements about exile in Paris as a kind of leveller – 'I proved, to my astonishment, to be as American as any Texas G.I.' – his short story in particular exposes the complex entanglements of race, nationality and privilege whilst at the same time questioning what it means to be American (*CE* 137). Baldwin's essay and short story pointedly draw attention to the privileges of American nationality. In 'Discovery', Baldwin states clearly that if the American artist 'were living there as a European, he would be living on a different and far less attractive continent', a comment that precedes his brief discussion of how an Algerian might feel in Paris (*CE* 141). In 'This Morning', the narrator recalls how 'I once thought of the North Africans as my brothers', but has since learnt that his American identity runs deeper than any sense of African heritage (*GTMTM* 157).[13] In contrast to the North Africans who want to overrule their colonizers, the narrator is grateful to his adopted nation who 'saved . . . [his] life' (*GTMTM* 158). And yet 'This Morning', with its multi-national cast explodes the myths of nationality as a straightforward acquisition or birth-right. The narrator's recollection of returning to New York is strongly evocative of the immigrants' arrival at Ellis Island. Paul, the narrator's son, is half-American, half-Swedish but has never been to the United States and speaks with a French accent; Harriet, the narrator's wife is described as 'abnormally dark for a Swedish girl' and she starts to pick up an Alabama drawl (*GTMTM* 149). And the narrator – unnamed throughout – stars in a film as the son of a French *colon* and Martinique woman. 'There's no place like home' the narrator hears a passenger say as they arrive in New York. Or perhaps, Baldwin seems to be saying, there is no place that *is* home (*GTMTM* 164).

In *James Baldwin's Turkish Decade*, Magdalena Zaborowska persuasively argues that Baldwin's interrupted decade in Turkey (1961–1971) dramatically shaped his writing, adding what she terms 'an increasingly transnational perspective' to his fiction and non-fiction.[14] During the ten years that he spent intermittent intervals in Turkey, Baldwin finished or wrote a number of works – including *Another Country*, *The Fire Next Time*, *Blues For Mister Charlie*, *Going to Meet the Man*, *Tell Me How Long the Train's Been Gone*, *One Day When I was Lost*, and *No Name in the Street*. Whilst in Turkey Baldwin also directed a critically acclaimed production of the Canadian playwright John Herbert's *Fortune and Men's Eyes* (1964), a success that American critics knew little about.[15] Zaborowska's book illuminates the impact of Turkey on Baldwin's life and work. As Baldwin himself noted, Turkey stands at the crossroads of Europe and Asia; thus, as he told Ida Lewis, 'During my stay in Istanbul I learned a lot about dealing with people who are neither Western nor Eastern'. Living in Turkey gave Baldwin a new perspective. Living amongst people 'whom nobody cares about', 'You learn about the brutality and the power of the Western world' (*CWJB* 86).

Zaborowska's meticulous study of Baldwin's sojourn in Turkey encourages us to view Baldwin's work from an international, not just North American critical perspective, highlighting how his 'awareness of the imperial presence of the United States in the world and of global racism increased and sharpened while he was living in Turkey'.[16] Zaborowska's work is also a useful reminder of the ways in which his perspectives on transnational culture developed. If Baldwin was cautious about transnational black collaboration in the 1950s, his later work suggested the possibility of such a project. For some critics such as Ernest Champion, Baldwin's participation at the 1980 African Literature Association marked a turnaround in his otherwise cautious discussions of African kinship. In his encounter with the Nigerian writer, Chinua Achebe, Baldwin seems to have found companionship, despite the cultural and geographical differences. Commenting on Achebe's 1958 novel *Things Fall Apart*, Baldwin stated that 'I recognized everybody in it. And that book was about my father'.[17]

Although the Baldwin-Achebe encounter was a profound event, Baldwin's ideas of Africa had already started to shift by the late 1970s. In an interview with *Africa: International Business, Economic and Political Magazine* in 1978, he began to articulate the need and desire for a dialogic encounter between black Americans and Africans, stressing what he termed their 'cultural interdependence' (*CWJB* 169). Here Baldwin explicitly reworked his earlier notion that the 'only thing that really unites all black men everywhere is, as far as I can tell, the fact that white men are on their necks' (*CWJB* 17). In the *Africa* interview Baldwin pointedly discussed a relationship that is 'much deeper than the common experience of colonialism or neo-colonialism', what he later termed 'cultural interplay' (*CWJB* 169). Noting how his nephew had found his visit to Africa 'tremendously liberating', Baldwin spoke of his hope for more cultural interaction between the US and Africa for the next generation. And as he stated in a later interview with Jordan Elgrably and George Plimpton, 'If I was twenty-four now, I don't know if and where I would go . . . I don't know if I would go to France, I might go to Africa' (*CWJB* 246).

In the Elgrably and Plimpton interview, Baldwin seems to revise his earlier insistence on the African American's disconnection from European culture that he had articulated in 'Stranger in the Village' (1953), a shift that had begun in *No Name in the Street*. In the earlier essay, Baldwin had written of how 'the most illiterate among them [the villagers] is related, in a way that I am not, to Dante, Shakespeare . . . Chartres . . .' (*CE* 121). In *No Name*, far from looking wistfully at European culture, Baldwin wrote that 'The South African coal miner, or the African digging for roots . . . have no reason to bow down before Shakespeare, or Descartes . . . or the Cathedral at Chartres' (*CE* 381). In the Elgrably-Plimpton interview, Baldwin states this position more clearly: 'Europe is no longer a frame of reference, a standard bearer, the classic model for literature and for civilization . . . When I was a kid, the world was white . . . and now it is struggling to *remain* white – a very different thing' (*CWJB* 246).

Baldwin's comments here and elsewhere in the last decade or so of his life suggest that his aesthetic and political outlook had shifted to include a broader, trans-cultural perspective. As Baldwin stated in the late 1970s, 'America is vast by itself, and yet the sense is that one no longer wishes to be isolated on the American continent', adding that 'we have to know what is going on in Africa and Africa has to know what is going on in Black America' (*CWJB* 169). In 'Stranger in the Village', Baldwin wrote that 'This world is white no longer, and it will never be white again' (*CE* 129). Between this prophetic comment in 1953 and the changing world order of the cold war and Vietnam, Baldwin's views evolved and developed, as is demonstrated most notably in his fierce critique of America's global imperialism. As he wrote in *No Name*, 'the cultural pretensions of history are revealed as nothing less than a mask for power', citing 'Shell, Texaco, Coca-Cola, the Sixth Fleet' as agents of power (*CE* 382). As I discuss in the following chapter, Baldwin was keenly aware of the ways in which the struggles for civil rights during the 1950s and 60s were inextricably bound to wider issues surrounding power that went far beyond the boundaries of the US borders.

2

The Writer and the Civil Rights Movement

On 17 May 1963 James Baldwin appeared on the front cover of *Time Magazine*. The painting by the well-known artist Boris Chaliapin shows Baldwin looking out with furrowed brow under the banner 'Birmingham and Beyond: the Negro's Push for Equality'. Inside the magazine, a lengthy article, 'Nation: The Root of the Problem' focuses on Baldwin. The article claims that 'in the U.S. today there is not another writer – white or black – who expresses with such poignancy and abrasiveness the dark realities of the racial ferment in North and South'.[1] Baldwin, *Time Magazine* suggests, is *the* voice of the Civil Rights movement.

Baldwin's appearance on the cover of such a popular weekly is testament to his importance and significance in the popular imagination, not just as a writer but as a civil rights activist. That year, Martin Luther King, Jr, was the magazine's 'Man of the Year', but it was a rare feat for an African American to be on the cover of any major US publication in the early 1960s. Baldwin's third novel, *Another Country*, published in 1962, was the second best-selling novel of 1963 after William Golding's *Lord of the Flies*. In 1962 the *New Yorker* published a long two part essay, 'A Letter from a Region in My Mind' that was reprinted as *The Fire Next Time* the following year, a book that became one of the manifestos of the Civil Rights movement. Unlike Richard Wright, who remained in France, and Ralph Ellison, who believed that political involvement corroded artistic talent, Baldwin lent his support to numerous civil rights organizations, contributing articles and interviews to scores of publications.

The article in *Time Magazine*, while testifying to Baldwin's influence as writer at the height of his success, simultaneously authenticates and undermines the writer's role in the Civil Rights movement. 'He is not, by any stretch of the imagination', the unnamed author writes, 'a Negro leader'. The article makes it clear that Baldwin 'tries no civil rights cases in the courts'; he 'preaches from no pulpit, devises no stratagems for sit-ins, Freedom Riders or street marchers'. Baldwin, in other words, is not a lawyer, preacher or political organizer. What, then, was Baldwin's role? According to the article Baldwin was 'thrust from typewriter to rostrum' after *The Fire Next Time*, and yet the magazine piece struggles to locate the source or significance of the writer. 'Baldwin offers no easy answers for an end to the rage and the terror'; his hopes are changes, not in law, but morality. In contrast to the portrait of steely determination on the magazine's cover, the article describes Baldwin as 'a nervous, slight, almost fragile figure, filled with frets and fears'. More strikingly, he is, the article claims, 'effeminate in manner, drinks considerably ... and he often loses his audience with overblown arguments'.

The description of Baldwin as 'effeminate', anticipates the difficulties that the writer would face as an openly queer black writer and activist, at a moment when black radical politics was increasingly aligned with heterosexual masculinity. The term 'effeminate' is almost certainly a thinly veiled reference to his sexuality and the article implicitly suggests that he is out of place in the arena of civil rights activism. Baldwin was frequently referred to as 'Martin Luther Queen', in civil rights circles, with the implication that his sexuality hindered his impact and authority as an activist. The article seems to question his effectiveness even as an eloquent spokesman of the Civil Rights movement. His language, the article claims, is 'overblown', a further suggestion that his rhetoric lacks the authoritative and masculine logic of figures such as Malcolm X.

In what follows I trace Baldwin's involvement in the Civil Rights movement, both through his activism and his key writings, namely *The Fire Next Time*, *Tell Me How Long the Train's Been Gone* (1968) and his long essay *No Name In the Street* (1972), also drawing on his play, *Blues for Mister Charlie* (1964) and his short story 'Going to Meet the Man' (1965). As

I argue, Baldwin's contributions were by no means symbolic as I later show through an overview of the writer's considerable FBI file. The FBI dossier, though full of mistakes, is also a useful biography of Baldwin's political activities. The files document his commitment to the Civil Rights movement and they also attest to the Bureau's perception of Baldwin as an influential and disruptive figure during the 1960s.

BALDWIN'S EARLY ESSAYS ON THE MOVEMENT

In *No Name in the Street*, a long reflective essay on the movement, Baldwin recalls the moment that propelled him to leave Paris in order to 'pay his dues'. 'Facing us, on every newspaper kiosk', Baldwin recalls, 'were photographs of fifteen-year-old Dorothy Counts being reviled and spat upon by the mob as she was making her way to school in Charlotte, North Carolina' (*CE* 383). Counts was one of the first black students to enter the recently desegregated school of Harry Hiding High School; on her first day she was greeted by white students screaming at her and hurling rocks. In Baldwin's recollection, he sees the brutal visual image of a young black student attacked as he is 'meandering' with other black writers on his way to lunch while covering the first International Congress of Black Writers and Artists at the Sorbonne (*CE* 383). Baldwin is in fact wrong about the dates: the Congress of Black Writers and Artists took place in 1956 nearly a year before the photograph of Counts, and yet his linking of the two moments is significant and symbolic. For Baldwin the iniquities of the civil rights battlefields were far more pressing concerns than the development of an international black aesthetic, where unhurried lunches in Paris are far removed from the harsh realities of the American South. Baldwin recalls seeing Counts's photograph in a 'tree-shaded boulevard', in Paris, a safe and genteel environment, far removed from the 'strange fruit' on the poplar trees that Billie Holiday evoked so disturbingly or Baldwin's description in 'Nobody Knows My Name' of the red soil of Georgia, stained 'from the blood that had dripped down from these trees' (*CE* 198).

Baldwin's first trips to the American South were in 1957,

where he visited Birmingham, Little Rock and Atlanta. He wrote probing accounts of these visits, which were arranged with the financial support of *Partisan Review* and *Harper's*, and republished as 'A Fly in Buttermilk' (1958) and 'Nobody Knows My Name: A Letter from the South' (1959). In his first published essay, reprinted in his second collection of essays *Nobody Knows My Name: More Notes of a Native Son* (1961), Baldwin paints a vivid picture of the South, an area of the United States that he had never before visited. Baldwin writes that the South 'frightened' him; it was a hostile territory in which a queer black northern intellectual felt out of place, a point he would iterate in *No Name* where he recalls that 'I doubt that I really knew much about terror before I went South' (*CE* 187, 388).

In 'A Fly' Baldwin interviews an unnamed fifteen-year-old African American student who has enrolled at a white school. Anticipating his powerful letter to his nephew, James, in *The Fire Next Time*, Baldwin ponders the effects of integration and racism on this young student who deals with the threat of violence by white students through '[p]ride and silence' (*CE* 193). Baldwin's essays on the Civil Rights movement are characterized by a drive to understand the effects of racism on both blacks and whites, and here he seems determined to understand the psychology of the white principal. Rather than demonizing the teacher, Baldwin exposes the complexity of segregation, describing the principal as 'a very gentle and honorable man' (*CE* 194). For Baldwin, the principal was blinded by his refusal or inability to see African Americans, just as segregation 'has allowed white people . . . to *create*, in every generation, only the Negro they wished to see' (*CE* 195).

In 'Nobody Knows My Name', Baldwin reflects on the South as the 'Old Country', a territory both familiar and hostile to the northern African American, and in particular to the writer who was 'but one generation removed from the South' (*CE* 199). During his visit to Atlanta and Charlotte, North Carolina, Baldwin continues his discussion of inte-gration and is at pains to point out that the South is a varied and complex environment. He considers the black middle class from Atlanta, cut off from both white and black worlds and, as Lynn Scott has noted, astutely anticipates the ways in which southern governors would attempt to delay the process of integration.[2] Baldwin's writing here dances between prescient and probing social and political observations to lyrical and disturbing images of the psyche of the American South. In 'Nobody', Baldwin picks up on the hidden sexual past of the South in the landscape, reading into it the past and present acts of violence and desire. The essay is remarkable for the way that Baldwin picks apart the 'bitter interracial history', where desire is enacted under the cover of night, linked in the writer's description, to 'unspeakable longings' where the master raped his slave (CE 203, 204). In Baldwin's description of race relations in the South, it is not simply a matter of hate but a complex entanglement of covert desire and guilt, frequently resulting in violence, with the 'black man, sexless, hanging from a tree' (CE 204).

Baldwin's second visit to the South was in 1960 shortly after the first wave of sit-ins, sparked by four black students who sat in a segregated lunch counter on 1 February in Greensboro, North Carolina and shortly after the formation of the Student Non-Violent Coordinating Committee (SNCC), an organization to which he lent his support. Baldwin's two essays – 'They Can't Turn Back' for *Mademoiselle* and 'The Dangerous Road Before Martin Luther King' for *Harper's* are respectively penetrating accounts of the struggles for desegregation in Tallahassee, Florida, and an insightful account of King's role in the South. Baldwin's essays mark a development in his non-fiction, characterized by his positions as reporter, witness and participant. In 'They Can't Turn Back', Baldwin explores the complexity of race relations in the South, a system of 'cabala' that operates in an unspoken system of 'signs and symbols', where everyone knows their place (CE 622). As Baldwin reflects on what the students hope to achieve, he contends that they want 'nothing less than a total revision of the ways in which Americans see the Negro'. Crucially, in what would become a Baldwinian refrain, this process is inextricably connected to 'a total revision of the ways in which Americans see themselves' (CE 623). This point would become even clearer in Baldwin's later essays. White people, Baldwin wrote in 'My Dungeon Shook' (later published as *The Fire Next Time*) are 'still trapped in a history which they do not understand'; equality and integration will only be realized when there is collective action (*CE* 294).

Baldwin's second essay about his trip to the South in 1960, 'The Dangerous Road Before Martin Luther King', is an intimate portrait of the civil rights leader whom the writer had met on his first visit to the South. Baldwin notes that King is not pious or self-important but 'a man solidly anchored in those spiritual realities concerning which he can be so eloquent' (*CE* 639). After hearing King preach in Montgomery, Baldwin reflects on the role of the church in the movement, a theme he would return to in his play, *Blues for Mister Charlie*. Baldwin reflects on the power of King's sermons, writing that 'the great emotional power and authority of the Negro church was being put to a new use', adding that 'it had acquired a new power' (*CE* 643). Baldwin suggests that while the church as a whole was not embracing the changes needed to fight racial inequality, King's political and spiritual charisma was reinvigorating the battle for civil rights.

'The Dangerous Road' is more than a sharply focused snapshot of King: by comparing King's reputation in 1957 and 1960, Baldwin picks up on the mounting criticism of King's strategies as a leader, capturing him 'in the center of an extremely complex cross fire' (*CE* 646). Baldwin's essay anticipates the ways in which the movement would shift from its focus in the South (characterized by King's philosophy of non-aggression) to the more radical northern politics of action led by Malcolm X. In 'The Dangerous Road', Baldwin situates the difficulties facing King in the history of black American leaders, presciently noting that 'white men find King dangerous', but also 'many Negroes also find King dangerous' (*CE* 652). Here Baldwin's essay seems to unwittingly anticipate his own pulls as artist and spokesman which would characterize much of his writing and interviews from the mid-to late 1960s.

BALDWIN AS CIVIL RIGHTS PARTICIPANT

Baldwin was arguably the most eloquent and well known voice of the Civil Rights movement, where he was not just a reporter but, to use his preferred term, a 'witness' to the struggles for racial equality. Despite his participation in the movement, there are few substantial accounts of his political activism, a point that Carol Polsgrove notes in *Divided Minds: Intellectuals and the Civil Rights Movement* (2001).[3] Aside from David Leeming's biography there are few substantial accounts of Baldwin in the history of US civil rights and it is his FBI file, active between 1960 and 1974, that outlines the extent of the writer's political activities. The FBI files are not always accurate or reliable. Throughout the 1700 or so pages, there are numerous mistakes that undermine the status of the files as history or fact. Baldwin's date of birth, for example, is frequently incorrect; at one point the Bureau seems to believe that he is married to his sister and the titles of his widely available books are frequently incorrect – as in the cases of *Go Tell it to the Mountain* and *Another World*. Yet I would suggest that the FBI files nonetheless serve several purposes. First, they give us a clear indication of the Bureau's assessment of Baldwin's radical presence during the 1960s. Second, while much of the information is incorrect, the unnamed agents frequently collected newspaper clippings about Baldwin in addition to information about this political activity. Thus the files become a useful resource, fleshing out the writing on Baldwin's contributions to the Civil Rights movement.

On 18 April 1972 an unnamed agent concludes that Baldwin, 'due to his position as an author, is likely to furnish aid or other assistance to revolutionary elements because of his sympathy and/or ideology' (FBI Files 1595).[4] The assessment of Baldwin's radical status seems surprising, given the author's relatively quiet literary output by the early 1970s. Nonetheless the entry illustrates several points: first, writers were deemed radical and dangerous to the FBI, and second, support of civil rights activity was viewed as tantamount to civil disobedience. As Natalie Robins has shown in her comprehensive account of the FBI's surveillance of writers during the 1950s and 1960s, Hoover 'sought to pin a Red label on anyone who demanded equal rights for blacks, and all politically active blacks were considered security threats'.[5]

Baldwin's file was opened after he supported the Fair Play for Cuba Committee (FPCC), an organization set up by Vincent

T. Lee in 1960 to petition an end to the United States' economic boycott of Cuba. Although Baldwin's involvement with the FPCC was brief, his signature unwittingly alerted the Bureau to his radical potential, resulting in a dossier of over 1700 pages. Surveillance on Baldwin stepped up after the writer arranged to meet with Robert Kennedy on 24 May 1963. Baldwin brought along a group of his friends, including the actor Harry Belafonte, the sociologist Kenneth Clark and the playwright Lorraine Hansberry. Also present was Jerome Smith, a member of the New Orleans chapter of the Congress of Racial Equality (CORE) who was badly beaten during the Freedom Rides.

The meeting, as Kenneth Clark recorded in an article in the *New York Post* (which was clipped to Baldwin's FBI file) was not a success. Baldwin was frustrated at the way in which the Kennedy administration seemed unable or unwilling to listen to the concerns of the civil rights participants, one of the reasons he had brought along Smith who claimed he would not fight for his country while he remained a second-class citizen. Kennedy could not understand the grounds of Smith's argument, drawing parallels between slaves in America and the ways in which his Irish ancestors had faced discrimination in the US. Despite the consensus that the meeting was a failure in terms of the implementation of change, it demonstrates Baldwin's willingness to get involved in civil rights, not just as a writer, but as a participant. At the same time, Baldwin had his detractors who questioned his suitability as a spokesman for the movement. Harold Cruse, for example, in the *The Crisis of the Negro Intellectual* (1967) flagged the writer's 'failure to discuss the racial conflicts either in terms of possible practical solutions, or in terms of American economic or social realities'. Cruise, in an echo of the rhetoric employed in the 1963 *Time* magazine article, points to Baldwin's 'intellectual inconsistencies', and to the 'incoherence and emotionalism of his line of argument'.[6] Cruse's assessment of Baldwin is ungenerously phrased and yet he is right to suggest that the writer was less attuned to the finer details of strategy and organization. Baldwin was much more concerned with the moral complexities of racial inequality and in fact repeatedly shrugged off the label of spokesman or leader. 'I have never seen myself as a spokesman', Baldwin told Julius Lester, adding that 'A spokesman assumes he is speaking for others. I never assumed . . . that I could' (*CWJB* 226).

Baldwin's FBI files show the extent of his commitment to the movement, whether he was granting interviews, delivering speeches, writing articles or appearing on television. He was, for example, an active contributor to, and supporter of, the journal *Freedomways: A Quarterly Review of the Negro Freedom Movement*, a publication that was on the FBI's radar. In 1964 one of the reasons for keeping Baldwin on the FBI's Security Index is his 'personal involvement in the current civil rights struggle', not just 'the inflammatory nature of his writings'(FBI Files 393). A 1964 comment by an FBI operative concludes that Baldwin's file 'clearly depicts [the] subject as a dangerous individual who could be expected to commit acts inimical to the national defense and public safety of the United States in time of an emergency' (FBI Files 230). Baldwin's radicalism, however, was clearly hard to gauge, illustrated by the conclusion that the writer is 'against all forms of violence and shedding blood' (FBI Files 308).

THE FIRE NEXT TIME AND *NO NAME IN THE STREET*

The FBI's confusing portrait of Baldwin as both 'a dangerous individual' and one against violence reflects Baldwin's own shifts in rhetoric as the 1960s progressed. In *No Name in the Street*, Baldwin casts his eye over the ways in which the momentum and tactics of the Civil Rights movement changed; how it shifted from strategies of non-violent action to the radicalism of the Black Power movement. Or, as Baldwin puts it, 'the photograph of Angela Davis [imprisoned in 1970] has replaced the photograph of Dorothy Counts' (*CE* 384).

As Baldwin recalls in *No Name*, he was profoundly affected by the assassinations of Malcolm X in 1965 and Martin Luther King, Jr in 1968. Baldwin's long essays on the Civil Rights movement, *Fire* and *No Name*, published nearly a decade apart, offer a useful overview of the writer's shifting views on how racial equality might be achieved. Both essays are journeys, temporally and geographically, and the essays, which are discursive, personal and political, map out the movement's shifts in strategy and tactics. In *Fire*, Baldwin considers the role of the church and then the nation of Islam and in *No Name* he turns to an insightful discussion of the Black Panther Party for Self Defense. If *Fire* offers little in the sense of concrete solutions to the racial nightmare confronting America, then *No Name* signals a shift in Baldwinian rhetoric, as the author ponders the deaths of King and Malcolm X in the hangover of the Black Power movement.

The Fire Next Time is more than just a civil rights manifesto: it begins with a letter to his nephew, also called James, counselling his sister's son to 'accept them [white people] and accept them with love' (CE 293–4). The short letter is by no means a call to simply turn the other cheek: Baldwin makes it clear to his nephew that black identity and self-worth has 'been deliberately constructed to make you believe that what white people say about you' (CE 293). And yet *Fire* is characterized by a tone of optimism. For Baldwin, it is possible 'to end the racial nightmare . . . and change the history of the world', if 'the relatively conscious whites and the relatively conscious blacks . . . like lovers, insist on, or create, the consciousness of the others' (CE 346–7). Baldwin does not suggest that this is a straightforward process and is clear that the alternative vision is apocalyptic ('*No more water, the fire next time!*) and yet this possibility of transformation is far removed from the sense of hopelessness in *No Name* (CE 347).

Nearly a decade after *Fire*, Baldwin's writing is characterized by a very different kind of language. Gone are the references to love, a word that became increasingly anachronistic in the face of mounting violence as the Black Power movement gathered momentum from the mid-1960s. Although Baldwin had made it clear in *Fire* that he meant love 'in the tough and universal sense of quest and daring and growth', his later tone of gritty optimism had been toned down by the time *No Name* was published (CE 341). 'Since Martin's death in Memphis', Baldwin writes in *No Name*, 'something has altered in me, something has gone away' (CE 357). As he reflected on how the battlegrounds had shifted from the dignity of Rosa Parks to the militaristic force of the Black Panthers, Baldwin concluded that 'it was inevitable that the fury would erupt' (CE 455).

Fire is written with a piercing intensity, casting a spotlight over the American psyche, probing into the failures of the American nation, both black and white. The last third of 'Down at the Cross' is a relentless examination of white America's failure to confront the past and present of black America – 'of rope, fire, torture, castration, infanticide, rape' (*CE* 342). Even God is held up to scrutiny. If God cannot make us 'larger, freer, and more loving', Baldwin writes, 'then it is time we got rid of Him' (*CE* 314). If Baldwin questions the validity and efficacy of the black church, he is still cautious in his assessment of the nation of Islam. For Baldwin, the rhetoric of the nation of Islam 'is nothing new', a variation on a theme that he had heard as child, where his father forbade him from having white friends (*CE* 325). After taking his leave of the Honorable Elijah Muhammad, Baldwin describes how he met up with some 'white devils' in a bar, a detail that is both cheekily irreverent and also telling, suggesting that the author has no intention of giving up his white friends, or, for that matter, alcohol. Though Baldwin later poses the question 'Do I really *want* to be integrated into a burning house?' the question is less for Baldwin about separatism (something he dismisses) but about dousing water on the house to make it habitable. Baldwin admires the strategies of the nation of Islam but charges them with failing to recognize that black Americans have been forged in the American crucible; that African Americans do not belong to Islam or Africa. 'An invented past can never be used', Baldwin writes, urging black Americans to confront their history in the United States (*CE* 333).

No Name, published as the momentum of the Black Power movement dissipated, looks back, for the most part, rather than forward. In contrast to the steely tone of hope in *Fire*, Baldwin's tone has shifted: the essay reads in part as a post-mortem of the movement's optimism that was instilled by the leadership of Malcolm X and Martin Luther King. After their assassinations in 1965 and 1968 respectively, Baldwin wrote that 'The Western party is over, and the white man's sun has set' (*CE* 475). *No Name* is by no means a hagiography of King; Baldwin's essay charts the growing disillusionment with King's tactics of non-violence, which seemed increasingly unachievable. Baldwin concludes that the 1963 march on Washington was 'a sell-out', adding that 'it seemed clear that we had merely postponed . . . the hour of dreadful reckoning' (*CE* 440). Baldwin's essay not only captures the shift in the Civil Rights movement from King to Malcolm X but turns towards an advocacy of black radical politics. In a curious twist, Baldwin employs the heterosexist masculine rhetoric of black radical writers such as Eldridge Cleaver, whose 1968 collection of essays, *Soul on Ice*, accused the older writer of being 'a reluctant black' and 'a white man in a black body'.[7] In Baldwin's writing, Cleaver continues, we find a 'total hatred of the blacks', suggesting that his sexuality rendered him less authentically black.[8] In *No Name*, Baldwin describes Malcolm X as 'a virile impulse', adding that Cleaver, who had attacked him with such venom, 'was vulnerable and rare' (*CE* 412, 459). Baldwin, whom the FBI concluded was against bloodshed, now wrote that his life had 'more than once depended on the gun in a brother's holster' (*CE* 472).

The reasons for Baldwin's shift in tone and style are not straightforward but *No Name* is punctuated with references to the author's self-awareness of his uncertain reputation in the movement. Baldwin's detailed descriptions of his visits to the South (trips he had already written about) place him as witness and participant: 'I will always consider myself among the greatly privileged', he writes, 'because, however inadequately, I was there' (*CE* 398–9). And yet, as Baldwin acknowledges throughout the essay, the very act of writing about the movement means that he is observer rather than activist. '[O]ne marches in Montgomery', Baldwin wryly notes, 'to sell one's books' (*CE* 364). Baldwin is acutely aware of his status as celebrity: from his encounter with a childhood friend who asks for his suit (a suit worn at the funeral of Martin Luther King) to a muted sense of embarrassment – or at least defensiveness – that he was in Hollywood when King was murdered. Baldwin had in fact been working on a film about Malcolm X (a project from which he withdrew) but his sojourn in a Beverly Hills hotel is contrasted sharply with the violence of the South and the murder of King in particular.

Baldwin's involvement with black radical politics was not just symbolic. As his FBI files attest, as well as strident views in *No Name*, Baldwin was no arm-chair agitator. He campaigned long and hard for the release of Tony Maynard, an African American wrongly imprisoned in Germany (and the inspiration for Fonny in *If Beale Street Could Talk*) and he worked on numerous occasions with the Black Panthers. As I explore through a brief reading of his last novel of the 1960s, *Tell Me How Long the Train's Been Gone*, the dual roles of celebrity and activist were fraught with difficulties. Baldwin was increasingly viewed as anachronistic by young black radicals at the same time that critics began to pronounce his artistic decline.

BALDWIN'S FICTIONAL ACCOUNTS OF THE MOVEMENT

I want to conclude with brief readings of three accounts of the Civil Rights movement in Baldwin's fictional work: his play, *Blues for Mister Charlie*, his short story 'Going to Meet the Man', and his critically neglected novel, *Tell Me How Long the Train's Been Gone*. These three pieces illustrate Baldwin's meditations on the shift in black politics during the 1960s; the tensions between non-violence and more radical action; and the ways in which racism is inextricably linked to the sexualization of the black body. Most of Baldwin's novels refer, at least in passing, to the horrors of racial inequality. In *Go Tell it on the Mountain*, for example, there are brief but striking images of a castrated black Second World War veteran and the demise of Richard, who is falsely arrested and then commits suicide (*GTM* 164, 202). In *Another Country*, there are flashbacks to the South where Rufus recalls his time in a boot camp and the beating he received from a white police officer (*AC* 22). In his last novel, *Just Above My Head*, Baldwin recounts the disturbing disappearance of Peanut, who is kidnapped by white racists in the South, never to be seen again (*JAMH* 463). In Baldwin's novels, racism is not only dangerous but deadly, tearing apart the black male body or effacing it completely.

According to Stanley Crouch, *Blues for Mister Charlie*, which was performed four months after the assassination of John F. Kennedy, fuelled debates about the question of non-violence, while for Amiri Baraka, the play 'announced the Black Arts

Movement'.[9] 'We've been demonstrating – *non-violently* – for more than a year now', Lorenzo declares in Act One, 'and all that's happened is that now they'll let us into the crummy library downtown' (*BFMC* 4). Dedicated to the memory of the murdered activist Medgar Evers and the children murdered in Birmingham in 1963, Baldwin's play, set in the fictional southern town of Plaguetown, draws on the murder of the fifteen-year-old Emmett Till, a northern teenager lynched for allegedly whistling at a white girl. The play is a dramatic exploration of a pivotal moment in the history of US civil rights when southern activists grew increasingly disillusioned with the role of the church during mounting violence. 'It's that damn white God', Lorenzo tells Mother Henry, 'that's been lynching us and burning us and castrating us and raping our women' (*BFMC* 4). After Richard is murdered by Lyle, a white store-owner, for insulting his wife, Richard's father, the preacher Meridian, must come to terms with his faith. The play concludes with the suggestion that the church alone is not able to deal with the plague of racism: 'it all began with the Bible and the gun', Meridian states at the end of the play, 'Maybe it will end with the bible and the gun' (*BFMC* 120).

Baldwin's play makes it clear that Richard, like Emmett Till, was murdered because of the perceived sexual threat of black men. 'Why have you spent so much time trying to kill me?' Richard asks Lyle as he is shot, 'Why are you always trying to cut off *my* cock?' (*BFMC* 120). Much of Baldwin's writing explores the complex entanglement of sex and racism. In *No Name*, for example, Baldwin makes it clear that it was 'the white men, who invented the nigger's big black prick', suggesting the ways in which racism is inextricably bound to a fear and desire of the black male body (*CE* 392). Nowhere is this theme more explicit than his short story 'Going to Meet the Man', the title of his only collection of stories, published in 1965. Set in the South and told through the eyes of Jesse, the town's white sheriff, 'Going to Meet the Man', explores how the protagonist's racism is deeply connected to the sexual arousal that he feels for black women. Jesse recalls how his father took him to see a lynching when he was eight years old, a spectacle that terrified but also enthralled him. As the black man is burnt and castrated, the young Jesse 'began to feel a joy he had never felt before', realizing that 'At that moment Jesse loved his father more than he had ever loved him' (*GTMTM* 250, 251). The story ends with the adult Jesse recollecting the lynching, arriving at a state of sexual arousal, telling his wife, Grace, that 'I'm going to do you like a nigger' (*GTMTM* 252).

Baldwin's short story reveals that racism operates along complex circuits of desire and revulsion. Echoing Frantz Fanon's observation that the white gaze transforms black men so that '[h]e is turned into a penis. He *is* a penis', Hall Montana, Baldwin's narrator in *Just Above My Head*, bemoans that 'its color *was* its size' (*JAMH* 105).[10] Baldwin's critique of the ways in which black male sexuality was portrayed in the public imagination put him at odds with a number of younger black radicals. For Cleaver in particular, black American men needed to reclaim their patriarchal 'rights' that had been denied to them during slavery. In order to redress this imbalance, Cleaver and other black radicals set out to portray the black male as heterosexual and hyper-masculine, an image which would be critiqued by Michele Wallace in her long essay, *Black Macho and the Myth of the Superwoman* (1979).

I want to conclude by examining Baldwin's neglected novel, *Tell Me How Long the Train's Been Gone*, published in 1968. Few reviewers took to Baldwin's last novel of the 1960s, the story of a black American actor, Leo Proudhammer. Eliot Fremont-Smith's coruscating review, which described the novel as 'a disaster in virtually every particular – theme, characterization, plot, rhetoric', was typical.[11] Yet the novel is important especially because it illuminates and examines Baldwin's problematic roles as artist and activist during the Civil Rights movement, particularly in the ways that Leo is torn – like Baldwin – between his artistic and political responsibilities.

Tell Me How Long is arguably Baldwin's least hopeful novel. There is no solace in religion, seen in the book as outmoded and ineffectual in the battle for racial equality. The novel explores the rise of black radicalism, where young black men dress 'in their Castro berets' (*TMHL* 382). These radicals do not read the bible but instead devour works by Camus, Fanon and Mao in what is a clear allusion to the stylized outfits of the Panthers and their Marxist ideology.

Despite its laboured prose and unwieldy plot, *Tell Me How Long* is also notable for how Baldwin explores Leo's sexual relationship with Black Christopher, a much younger black radical. Published the same year as Cleaver's *Soul on Ice*, *Tell Me How Long* suggests an alternative to the patriarchal heterosexuality that characterized much of the black radical rhetoric of the mid to late 1960s. In *Tell Me How Long* Baldwin explores the ways in which male companionship, love and eroticism are entangled, challenging the homophobia and heterosexism that characterizes much Black Nationalist writing. In Baldwin's novel, it is 'men, who are far more helpless than women'; they 'need each other as comrades', and 'need each other . . . in sum to be able to love women' (*TMHL* 81).

As I explore in the following chapter, there is a marked difference between Baldwin's discussion of sexuality in his fiction and his relative silence in his non-fiction, a feature which is notable in his essays on the Civil Rights movement. As one of the movement's most insightful and famous commentators, Baldwin apparently did not have the space to explore the complex entanglement of race and sexuality in his non-fiction. At the same time, as I explore in the next chapter, Baldwin did carve out a space to talk about race and sexuality in his pioneering fiction and a cluster of essays.

3

Racial and Sexual Difference

As the first openly queer major African American writer since the Harlem Renaissance, Baldwin's life and work paved the way for gay black writing. Prior to Baldwin's pioneering work, according to Joseph Beam, black American literature had been suffering 'a kind of 'nationalistic heterosexism'.[1] Beam's claim is corroborated by the testimonies of gay black artists such as Randall Kenan and Isaac Julien and also by a growing number of scholars who have challenged the critical divisions that have treated Baldwin's race and sexuality as somehow unconnected. As Andrea Lowenstein noted in a pioneering essay in 1980, 'One wonders whether, if Baldwin were *either* black or gay, more reviewers might be able to actually address his work itself'. Instead, Lowenstein argues, Baldwin's 'double minority status is so "threatening" that what is finally reviewed in the end is the critics' own fears and projections'.[2] Since the 1990s, however, with the emergence of queer theory and then black queer theory, critics including Emmanuel Nelson and Robert Reid-Pharr have highlighted the ways in which Baldwin's work explores the complex traffic of race, sexuality and masculinity, in particular foregrounding the 'double minority status' that Lowenstein addressed in Baldwin's racial and sexual identities. As Yasmin DeGout argues, Baldwin's fiction 'reveals him to be progenitor of many of the theoretical formulations currently associated with feminist, gay, and gender studies'.[3]

Despite his reputation as one of the most important gay black writers of the twentieth century, Baldwin himself rarely employed the terms gay, homosexual and bisexual. While his second novel, *Giovanni's Room* (1956) is rightly considered to be a major work of American homosexual literature, Baldwin instead stated that it 'is not about homosexuality'.[4] I argue in this chapter that Baldwin's comment in fact fits squarely with his complicated views on sexuality. 'The word gay', Baldwin told Richard Goldstein in 1985, 'has always rubbed me the wrong way. I never understood exactly what is meant by it', a view that he also forcefully echoed in an interview with James Mossman:[5]

> those terms, homosexual, bisexual, heterosexual, are 20th-century terms which, for me, have very little meaning. I've never, myself, in watching myself and watching other people, watching life, been able to discern exactly where the barriers were. (*CWJB* 54)

Asked by Goldstein whether he considered himself gay, Baldwin replied that he did not: 'I didn't have a word for it. The only one I had was homosexual and that didn't quite cover whatever it was I was beginning to feel'.[6]

As I illustrate with a reading of his essays on sexuality, followed by an examination of his fictional treatments of homosexuality and bisexuality, Baldwin's views complicate a reading of his work that tries to place him in any one category, including the position of a black queer writer. In fact there's an irony that Baldwin, the inspiration and progenitor of black queer writing, repeatedly steered readers away from the theme of homosexuality in his work, insisting on themes that continue to trouble literary critics such as love and spirituality.

BALDWIN'S ESSAYS ON HOMOSEXUALITY

Despite his reputation as one of the twentieth century's most important and pioneering homosexual writers only three of Baldwin's essays focus on sexuality. In fact Baldwin did not discuss his own sexuality until 1985 in an essay titled 'Here Be Dragons', also published as 'Freaks and the American Ideal of Manhood'. In 1949 Baldwin wrote 'Preservation of Innocence', an astonishingly bold essay that discusses homosexuality, masculinity and the American preoccupation with innocence. Challenging the old adage that homosexuality is 'unnatural', Baldwin argues that homophobia is the result of tensions between heterosexual couples which leads to heterosexual panic. In 1954 Baldwin wrote a review of André Gide's *Madeleine* (1952) in the *New Leader*, titled 'Gide as Husband and Homosexual' and republished in *Nobody Knows My Name* as 'The Male Prison'. Here Baldwin writes of how the French writer's homosexuality and Protestantism 'contributed most heavily to my dislike of Gide', adding that his sexuality 'was his own affair which he ought to have kept hidden from us', a comment he echoed some thirty years later (*CE* 231). In his interview with Goldstein, Baldwin curiously invokes the very Protestantism with which he chastised Gide, stating that his own sexuality was 'very personal, absolutely personal. It was really a matter between me and God'.[7]

Although Baldwin discussed his sexuality during a handful of interviews from the mid-1960s, the thirty year gap between essays on homosexuality (from 'The Male Prison' to 'Freaks') seems surprising, especially as his fiction, notably *Another Country* (1962), *Tell Me How Long the Train's Been Gone* (1968) and *Just Above My Head* (1979) foregrounds homosexual and bisexual relationships. On the one hand, as Baldwin suggested in his interviews with Mossman and Goldstein, the writer did not identify with a homosexual subculture; he grew up a generation before Stonewall, the 1969 riots that marked the start of the gay rights movement in the US. During his teenage years, as he recalled in 'Freaks', 'the queer – not yet gay – world was an even more intimidating area of this hall of mirrors', adding that 'the mirrors threw back only brief and distorted fragments of myself' (*CE* 823). Baldwin's account of what he called his 'season in hell' is a useful reminder that he grew up several generations before the emergence of black queer theory.

Later black gay artists such as Marlon Riggs have striven to show the absurdity of privileging either blackness or sexuality, illustrated by an exchange between a straight activist and an unnamed gay African American in Riggs's 1989 documentary *Tongues Untied*. 'Come the final throw-down', asks the activist, 'what is he first? Black or gay?' The response underscores the inextricability of race and sexuality: 'which does he value most. His left nut or his right?'[8] For Baldwin, however, whose writing was forged in a very different crucible, 'the sexual question comes after the question of color', as he explained to Richard Goldstein, a comment which in part explains the division in his essays between the subjects of race and homosexuality. On the few occasions that Baldwin discussed homosexuality in his essays, he rarely discussed blackness, as is illustrated by his two important essays in *Zero*, 'Everybody's Protest Novel', and 'Preservation of Innocence'. Published in the first and second issues of *Zero*, the first essay addresses race but does not mention homosexuality, just as 'Preservation' focuses on white literature and male desire for men.

In a discussion of *Giovanni's Room*, Baldwin recalled that it 'would have been quite beyond ... [his] powers' to include a black homosexual character in the mid-1950s, and yet the author continued to keep the two themes of race and sexuality in alcoves part (*CWJB* 239). According to Jerome de Romanet, Baldwin 'reserved the more public voice of spokesman (of the black community as a whole, of writers and artists) for his essays and formal addresses, while he often let his fictional characters discuss the more private issues of sexual politics and preference'.[9] De Romanet's comment is a useful reminder of the various roles that Baldwin occupied as artist, public intellectual and civil rights spokesman. In essays such as *The Fire Next Time* (1963), a key text of the Civil Rights movement, Baldwin explored the psychological damage of racism on both blacks and whites. Written only a year after his controversial bestseller, *Another Country*, a novel which outraged many readers because of the graphic descriptions of bisexuality, *The Fire Next Time* foregrounds race with no mention of sexuality, supporting de Romanet's claim that Baldwin's fiction was the medium in which he explored sexual politics and preference.

Although Baldwin considered his sexuality a private matter, he was also openly queer, which left him vulnerable to attacks by younger black radicals such as Eldridge Cleaver who viciously attacked the older writer in *Soul on Ice* (1968). Here Cleaver fixates on Baldwin's sexuality, claiming that homosexuality is a sickness akin to baby rape.[10] For Cleaver and writers including Amiri Baraka, homosexuality was a 'white disease', an aberration that let down the race. Cleaver in particular wanted to reassert black masculinity through the Black Power movement; to make up for the disempowerment that black men had experienced during slavery and its legacy. The correlation between freedom and masculinity—what bell hooks termed 'freedom with manhood', left little room for women or gay men.[11] For Baldwin this hyper-masculinity was dangerous, not only because it excluded many African Americans, but because it perpetuated white myths of black sexual appetite. Whereas Cleaver celebrated 'the walking phallus of the Supermasculine Menial' (i.e. male black American), Baldwin repeatedly critiqued and repudiated what he saw as dangerous images of black male sexuality. 'It is still true alas', Baldwin wrote in 1961, 'that to be an American Negro male is also to be a kind of walking phallic symbol: which means one pays, in one's personality, for the sexual insecurity of others' (CE 269–70).

Cleaver's highly publicized attack on Baldwin in Soul on Ice almost certainly had a profound effect on the older writer. As late as 1984 Baldwin still spoke of trying to 'undo the damage' that Cleaver had caused (CWJB 252). According to Henry Louis Gates, Jr, Baldwin's essays shifted in tone and content after the publication of Soul on Ice. Gates argues that Baldwin's essays 'came to represent his official voice, the carefully crafted expression of the public intellectual, James Baldwin'.[12] As Dwight McBride persuasively argues, Baldwin increasingly adopted the voice of 'representative race man', which in turn led to a silencing – or at least dilution – of his depictions of homosexuality.[13]

BALDWIN'S FICTION

In contrast to his essays, Baldwin pioneered fictional accounts of homosexuality and bisexuality in his fiction. Giovanni's Room, for example, was one of the first successful treatments of homosexuality in American fiction. Published in 1956, Baldwin's novel had few if any precedents other than Gore Vidal's 1948 novel, The City and the Pillar. And yet, as I want to argue, Baldwin rarely offers straightforwardly sympathetic accounts of queer desire. Some critics such as the black science fiction writer Samuel Delany have pointed out that Baldwin's portrayals of homosexuality were far from positive.[14] Whilst Delany acknowledges that Baldwin 'at least, *had* talked about it', displaying 'a certain personal honesty', he groups *Giovanni's Room* with other negative portrayals of homosexuality, such as the writing of Havelock Ellis.[15] Similarly, although Emmanuel Nelson has pioneered a re-examination of Baldwin's portrayals of homosexuality, he concludes that *Giovanni's Room* evinced a Baldwin who had 'not freed himself from the internalization of homophobic beliefs regarding the origins of male homosexual impulses'.[16] And finally, for Donald Gibson, '[t]he fact of the matter is that Baldwin's attitude toward homosexuality is decidedly critical'.[17]

In recent years few literary critics have picked up on Baldwin's at times uncomfortable representations of homosexuality and yet there are a number of instances where the writer makes a distinction between acceptable or unacceptable forms of sexual practice. In *Giovanni's Room*, David attempts to prove his heterosexual virility by contrasting his actions with those in the homosexual underworld. In contrast to Guillaume and Jacques, who are described as 'old theatrical sisters', David is introduced as 'this great American football player' (*GR* 34). Describing the locals of Guillaume's bar as '*les folles*', David is quick to distinguish himself from the homosexual crowd who 'would swoop in', 'screaming like parrots', referring to each other as 'she', crowding round the centre of gossip 'like a peacock garden . . . [that] sounded like a barnyard' (*GR* 30). In contrast, Giovanni and David do not spend time in the bar or mix with '*les folles*'. Giovanni is quick to compare what he deems as the camp frivolity of Guillaume and Jacques with his masculine love for David. It is '*they*', Giovanni declares, who are 'disgusting' (*GR* 105). And it is at the height of Giovanni's downfall that David notes, with disgust, that his former lover has begun to affect 'a fairy's mannerisms' (*GR* 139). Giovanni's move in the course of the novel, from a masculine homosexuality to that of the 'fairy', illustrates that the sexual roles are more fluid than David likes to imagine. Earlier in the novel Giovanni had described Guillaume as 'a disgusting old fairy', adding that he 'is not really a man at all' (*GR* 102, 62).

Baldwin of course may not have shared the views of his characters but there is a pattern in his fiction that suggests a dislike of camp and an approval of a more conventionally masculine homosexuality. In *Just Above My Head*, Baldwin is careful to distinguish Arthur from other homosexuals, adding that he was 'nobody's faggot', just as Eric, the hero of *Another Country* distances himself both from the 'raucous cries' of the 'birds of paradise', and the 'cemetery' of a gay bar (*JAMH* 30; *AC* 259, 327). In perhaps the most disturbing moment of *Giovanni's Room*, David encounters a transvestite in a bar. 'It looked like a mummy or a zombie', Baldwin writes, as though 'something walking after it had been put to death'. In Baldwin's description the transvestite is neither male nor female, a terrifying figure who 'moved with a horrifying lasciviousness' (*GR* 41). For Baldwin, like Vidal, who describes the 'strange womanish creatures' in *The City and the Pillar*, the transvestite is neither alive nor dead, a manifestation of Baldwin's warning in 'The Male Prison'.[18] Baldwin stated that Gide should have kept his sexuality hidden from readers and warned that 'today's unlucky deviate can only save himself by the most tremendous exertion of all his forces from falling into an underworld in which he never meets either men or women'. Crucially for Baldwin this means that 'the possibility of genuine human involvement has altogether ceased' (*CE* 234).

Much of Baldwin's fiction explores the ways in which his characters struggle to find connections with others – the human involvement that he described. For Baldwin, both heterosexual and homosexual relationships are damaged by 'a fear of anybody touching anybody'.[19] In order to redress this, Baldwin insists that we must overcome our 'fear of the flesh', 'a terror of human life, of human touch' (*CE* 385). As he repeatedly stated, '*Nobody* makes any connections', resulting in 'this truncated, de-balled, galvanized activity which thinks of itself as *sex*'.[20] In his fiction, homosexual men are at times the apotheosis of the very isolation that he warns against and yet, as I argue below, Baldwin's most hopeful descriptions of love are between men.

Although *Giovanni's Room* is Baldwin's most celebrated novel about homosexuality, his earlier fiction also explores the possibility of love between two teenage boys on the cusp of adulthood. In his short story 'The Outing', published in 1951 (collected in *Going to Meet the Man*) and in his first novel, *Go*

Tell it on the Mountain (1953), both set in the church, Baldwin explores what Michael Cobb describes as the author's 'queer evocation of conservative, Christian language'.[21] At first glance, 'The Outing' reads as a shorter version of *Go Tell it*. We quickly learn about the protagonist, Johnnie and his embittered relationship to his deacon father, Gabriel. Like *Go Tell it*, the narrative is framed by the church, but in 'The Outing' the plot unfolds on a church outing, as the congregation sail down the Hudson river.

The central difference between the two stories is in the close friendship that John (*Go Tell it*) and Johnnie ('The Outing') foster. In *Go Tell it*, John is strengthened by his admiration for Elisha's piety and manliness, 'wondering if he would ever be as holy as Elisha' (*GTM* 14). In 'The Outing', the central friendship is between David and Johnnie, names that suggest the biblical love between David and Jonathan, a theme explored in Baldwin's second novel through David and Giovanni (Italian for Jonathan). In *Go Tell it*, John discovers the possibility of redemption through love after a brief encounter with Elisha in the church. As John is cleaning the church, he wrestles with Elisha until the tussle becomes more and more intense. John watches 'the veins rise on Elisha's forehead and in his neck', feeling his 'breath' on him. Here Baldwin focuses on the bodies as they embrace one another in a place of worship: 'the odour of Elisha's sweat was heavy in John's nostrils . . . and John . . . was filled with a wild delight' (*GTM* 61). As the sweaty pair disentangle themselves after the climax of their struggle, Elisha asks 'I didn't hurt you none, did I', evoking a post-coital address and paralleling the tender whispers between David and Johnnie in 'The Outing': '"Who do you love?" he [David] whispered. "Who's your boy?" "You", he muttered fiercely, "I love you"' (*GTMTM* 39).

If Baldwin's early descriptions of love between men are framed through adolescents who have yet to navigate the complex adult world strewn with the expectations of piety and family, his later characters are almost all bisexual – or at least open to the idea of sex with men and women. In *Giovanni's Room*, David's engagement to Hella and seduction of Sue may well be desperate attempts to bolster his fragile heterosexuality but Giovanni, too, we learn, has been married, just as several characters in *Another Country* sleep with both men and women. Here I want to explore whether bisexuality most closely approximates Baldwin's vision of sexual love.[22] In particular, I want to consider whether bisexuality is Baldwin's key to the male prison, a condition that he refers to both in 'Preservation', and his essay on Gide. Given that so much of Baldwin's fiction is about the struggles to forge connections – whether between black and white, gay and straight, men and women – does bisexuality, offer the greatest chance for interpersonal communion?

In 'The Male Prison', Baldwin makes a veiled appeal to the idea of bisexuality. 'Men', Baldwin concludes, 'cannot live without women and women cannot live without men. . . . This door [communion with the sexes] . . . *must* be kept open, and none feel this more keenly than those on whom the door is perpetually threatening or has already seemed to close' (*CE* 234–5). Baldwin both condemns Gide's sacrifice of Madeleine – by forcing her to chastity – but also seems to suggest that the French writer *must* keep the door open to sexual relationships with women. Anticipating Leo in *Tell Me*, who explains the need for male companionship, 'in order to be able to love women', Baldwin suggests that the doors should never be closed (*TMHL* 81).

In contrast to homosexuality or heterosexuality, bisexuality arguably offers Baldwin a way out of the rigidly defining sexual identities that he so disdained. It is in 'Freaks and the American Ideal of Manhood' that he comes closest to advocating what would generally be construed as bisexuality in his non-fiction. Characteristically Baldwin avoids using the term 'bisexual', but uses the term 'androgynous', an adjective that Baldwin had tentatively used in *Another Country* to describe Eric (*AC* 324).[23] Baldwin ends 'Freaks' with an image of wholeness and neatness, of inter-related, inter-connected sexual, racial and gender axes:

> But we are all androgynous, not only because we are all born of a woman impregnated by the seed of man but because each of us, helplessly and forever, contains the other – male in female, female in male, white in black and black in white. We are a part of each other. (*CE* 828)

Baldwin's essay seems to suggest that categories and labels must be transcended, since we are all a part of one another. And yet, if Baldwin's point is that there is no such thing as an essential homosexual, heterosexual, masculine or feminine identity, then the rhetorical neatness of the ending of 'Freaks' too clinically ties up the remorse and agony that his writing elsewhere points to.

Earlier in 'Freaks', Baldwin suggests that sexuality is not something that you *are* but something that you do. In a recollection of his earliest sexual encounters, Baldwin stresses that 'male desire for a male roams everywhere', a phenomenon not limited to homosexual subcultures (*CE* 821). Indeed, Baldwin's long list of the men he encountered frames them in professions associated with heterosexual masculinity: these were men who 'looked like cops, football players, soldiers, sailors, Marines or bank presidents, admen, boxers, construction workers', adding that 'they had wives, mistresses and children' (*CE* 821). In *Another Country*, Baldwin more cynically describes a similarly mixed congregation of 'fathers, gangsters, football players, rovers', men who did not 'make love', but hid from their desires, surrendering to furtive fumbles in closeted rooms (*AC* 209).

I want to consider Baldwin's fictional accounts of bisexuality – or perhaps more accurately sexual fluidity – through brief readings of his third and last novels, *Another Country* and *Just Above My Head*. Like all Baldwin protagonists, Eric, as I discussed earlier, does not inhabit the gay subculture. In contrast to what is seemingly presented by Baldwin as the sterile stasis of homosexuality, bisexuality offers the possibility of a fluid desire; a desire symbolically represented by the transformation of Eric's wedding rings into cufflinks for Rufus, then earrings for Ida. Bisexual love also operates indirectly across social, politic and racial axes. As a young boy in Alabama, Eric experiences his first two loves with African American men, suggesting that Eric's sexuality enables him to be more open to racial difference. Baldwin suggests this further by describing how Eric owned a copy of *Native Son* as a young man, also noting that his first homoerotic encounter was with LeRoi, a working-class black American.

Baldwin's development of bisexuality in *Another Country* suggests, as Susan Feldman has noted, that the author 'does not conceive of identity in terms of essence'. Feldman convincingly argues that the figuration of bisexuality offers a model for Baldwin's understanding of identity because 'it registers the contingency at the heart of identity, and demands that we note the disjunctions among past, present, and future possibilities'.[24] Feldman's point serves to illuminate the important love-making between Eric and Vivaldo. As Eric makes love to Vivaldo, the latter imagines that he is both making love to Rufus, and also that he *is* Rufus, making love to Eric. As William Cohen states, '[t]his sexual connection generates an orgasmic concatenation of identities, whereby Vivaldo conceives of himself as simultaneously gay and straight, male and female, white and black'.[25] Vivaldo's lovemaking with Eric mimetically and posthumously fulfils his unrealized desire for Rufus. And yet the representations of fluid sexuality also raise several problematic questions. Why, for example, does Baldwin suggest that gay male desire can only be mediated indirectly to Rufus via Eric? Why is the novel's protagonist, mediator and even saviour, white and male? And if, as Cohen asks, the scene between Vivaldo and Eric does in fact trample down binaries and barriers, 'where does this disintegration lead?'[26]

One of the main problems of decoding Baldwin's message in *Another Country* and his wider view on sexuality – if indeed there is one – is that the author seems so ambivalent. In particular, Baldwin seems to be both drawn to and repelled by chaos: a space between boundaries that potentially offers a repudiation of identity categories as suggested by the end of 'Freaks'. *Another Country* is replete with descriptions of the ineffable: terrors that lie buried, all the more frightening because they are 'inexpressible' (*AC* 196). Eric's relationship with LeRoi is 'something unspeakable', something 'he could not, to save his soul, have named', just as he later feels 'unnamed forces within himself' (*AC* 202, 234). The references to Eric, it might be reasonably argued, refer to his 'unnameable' sexuality – the 'love that dare not speak its name' – but given Baldwin's dislike of the words homosexual/bisexual, this explanation falls short. Perhaps Baldwin does not want to reduce his characters' actions to one or other sexual practice – and so avoids framing their relationships explicitly. And yet this explanation still does not account for Baldwin's other references to the inexpressible. Both Eric and Cass fear the 'unanswerable and unimaginable riddles', as they meet beneath an 'unreadable' canvas that conveys 'unspeakable chaos' (*AC* 287, 396). What is happening to Cass, Eric suggests, is 'unspeakable', recalling Ida's singing, which 'no one has ever been able to name' (*AC* 396, 250).

Another Country remains a pioneering novel; it shocked a number of readers in the 1960s (including the FBI's director, J. Edgar Hoover) because of its graphic descriptions of interracial and homosexual sex. At the same time, it would not be until his final novel, *Just Above My Head*, that Baldwin described a loving sexual relationship between two African American men. I want to conclude with a brief overview of *Just Above My Head* to illustrate how it picks up and expands upon several key themes in his fictional work that I explore later in the book – namely the church and music. In his last novel, Baldwin not only uses gospel music as an expression of sexual love but a medium that sanctifies love between black men. When Arthur and Crunch play music together, the songs become a vicarious experience of spiritual sexual fulfilment:

> He [Arthur] paused again ... trusting every second of this unprecedented darkness, knowing Crunch and he were moving together, here, now, in the song, to some new place; they had never sung together like this before, his voice in Crunch's sound, Crunch's sound filling his voice. (*JAMH* 206)

The language is strongly evocative both of religious conversion ('some new place'), but also of sexual intimacy: a medium that allows the boys to enter and fill one another. As Arthur and Crunch sing gospel music, the music becomes a way of expressing the spirituality of their desire for one another, exemplified by Baldwin's nuancing of traditional songs: '*somebody touched me ... it must have been the hand of the Lord!*' (*JAMH* 207).

By framing same-sex relationships through gospel music, Baldwin redefines the boundaries between the sacred and the sacrilegious, also insisting on the purity of all love. According to Hall, the novel's narrator, music was for Arthur and Jimmy a way of placing and defining their love: music 'became for them, then, theirs, a sacrament, a stone marking a moment on their road: the point of no return, when they confessed to each other, astounded, terrified, but having no choice, in the hearing of men, and in the sight of God' (*JAMH* 575). As Hall marvels at the depth of love between Jimmy and Arthur, he is struck at how 'sacrilegious' his brother's love is; and yet, he is also struck by Arthur's response, 'which seemed to ring out over those apocalyptic streets' (*JAMH* 575). Love, often aided and nurtured through music, becomes the bedrock of Baldwin's vision of religious experience. Irrespective of class, gender or sexuality, love becomes, for Baldwin, a redemptive act. In *Just Above*, this is explicitly illustrated through Arthur's relationship with Crunch:

> And yet, he knows that, when he was happy with Crunch, he was neither guilty nor ashamed. He had felt a purity, a shining joy, as though he had been, astoundingly, miraculously blessed, and had feared neither Satan, man, nor God. He had not doubted for a moment that all love was holy. (*JAMH* 470–1)

As I explore in subsequent chapters, love in fact seems to serve as a model for Baldwin's religion. For it is 'love', Baldwin writes in his final novel, 'which is salvation' (*JAMH* 177).

4

Baldwin and Music

Although Baldwin would claim that he didn't 'know anything about music', his fiction and non-fiction is punctuated with references to the blues, gospel and jazz.[1] There are the titles of his short stories and novels: *Go Tell it on the Mountain* (a nineteenth century spiritual); *Just Above My Head* (a spiritual that Ida sings in *Another Country*); *If Beale Street Could Talk* (a reference to the home of the blues in Memphis), his most anthologized short story, 'Sonny's Blues', and the play *Blues for Mister Charlie* to name but a few. Many of Baldwin's fictional characters are musicians, whether singers (Ida in *Another Country*), jazz musicians (Rufus, also in *Another Country*), blues musicians (Luke in the play *The Amen Corner* and Frank in *Go Tell it on the Mountain*) or gospel singers (Arthur in *Just Above My Head*). In Baldwin's essays, too, he frequently invokes the names of jazz musicians and female blues singers, most notably Miles Davis, Ray Charles, Bessie Smith and Billie Holiday.

Baldwin would claim that he wanted to write the way jazz musicians sound but his writing on music suggests that the blues, jazz and gospel was much more than just an aesthetic or narrative device.[2] In his characterization of musicians, deployment of blues lyrics in his novels, and in his discussion of music in his non-fiction, blues, gospel and jazz become key political, cultural and even existential phenomena that are one of the cornerstones of his *oeuvre*. In his essay 'The Discovery of What it Means to Be an American', Baldwin recalls finishing *Go Tell it* in Switzerland in the foothills of a very different kind of mountain. Here Baldwin acknowledges his debt, not to his literary antecedents, but rather to the blues singer Bessie Smith.

It was Smith's 'tone and her cadence' that helped him 'dig back to the way I myself must have spoken when I was a pickaninny' (CE 138). In a 1973 interview, Baldwin would also talk of how Billie Holiday 'gave you back your experience. She refined it', Baldwin stated, 'and you recognized it for the first time . . .' (CWJB 155).

In other essays about music, such as his 1951 article 'Many Thousands Gone', Baldwin suggested not only that music helped him write, but also that music itself was the fundamental expression of black American culture. 'It is only in music', Baldwin wrote, 'that the Negro in America is able to tell his story' (CE 19). Here Baldwin anticipates the work of a number of Black Arts movement artists, including LeRoi Jones (now Amiri Baraka) by over a decade. In 'The Myth of a "Negro Literature"', published in 1963, Baraka argued that, since black American literature was based on white literary forms, no authentic African American literature had yet been written, arguing that blues and jazz was the truest expression of black American creativity.[3] Although Baldwin did not always privilege music over literature, he repeatedly turns to music as a source of political and creative inspiration. In an interview with the poet Nikki Giovanni, Baldwin remarked on the connections between music and literature in African American culture, drawing attention to the ways in which music has been a political tool as well as a cultural product:

> What we call black literature is really summed up for me by the whole career, let's say, of Bessie Smith, Ray Charles, Aretha Franklin, because that's the way it's been handed down . . . We had to smuggle information, and we did it through our music and we did it in the church. (AD 79)

But this smuggling, Baldwin suggests, continues: 'I will be able to accept critical judgments when I understand that they [white critics] understand Ray Charles', a statement evocative of Thelonius Monk's comment on bebop music: 'we're going to create something they can't steal because they [white folks] can't play it' (AD 84).[4] Similarly, in A Rap on Race, Baldwin again states, both how it is 'very sinister that no one knows what Ray Charles is singing about', but also raises the fundamental problem of communication. 'How', Baldwin asks the white anthropologist Margaret Mead, 'are we ever going to achieve some kind of language which will make my experience articulate to you and yours to me?'[5]

Baldwin's writing and comments at times seem to suggest that white Americans cannot really hear or play the blues. For James Lincoln Collier, Baldwin's review of his book *The Making of Jazz* (1979), suggested 'that jazz is black music, and the white man cannot really understand it, any more than he can understand what it means to be black in America'.[6] I want to suggest, however, that Baldwin's views on music and 'race' are not as straightforward as Collier suggests. In fact in 'The Uses of the Blues', an article that he wrote for *Playboy* in 1964, Baldwin makes it clear when he discusses black and white responses to music that he is 'not talking about race', but rather 'a social fact'.[7] For Baldwin, the expression of black American music comes from a particular place that is shaped by the confluence of history, politics and the related suffering of slavery and its legacies. Black American music, Baldwin writes, 'begins on the auction block'.[8] Baldwin suggests that whatever liberals claim, white Americans cannot understand the damage of slavery and its aftermath; or as Baldwin puts it succinctly, 'You don't know what the river is like or what the ocean is like by standing on the shore'.[9] Here Baldwin's writing on the black and white experiences of music veers towards – but never quite embraces – the notion that whites simply cannot understand or appreciate the blues. As Baldwin writes in *The Fire Next Time*, 'there is something tart and ironic, authoritative and double-edged', in jazz and the blues (*CE* 311). White Americans, Baldwin claims, 'do not understand the depths out of which such an ironic tenacity comes'(*CE* 311). Baldwin suggests that an experience of suffering is necessary in order to hear the full story that the blues singer tells. This experience is not *necessarily* racial, but it occurs more commonly among black Americans, though not always. In 'Sonny's Blues', the African American narrator does not at first understand the power of the music that his brother plays, suggesting that the experience of suffering and understanding can be intra-racial. Baldwin suggests that not all African Americans appreciate the blues, just as the white bisexual character Eric in *Another Country* is able to hear the pain and craft of Bessie

Smith. As Baldwin wrote in *The Fire Next Time*, the only hope of progress is for a white American 'to become black himself, to become a part of that suffering and dancing country . . .' (*CE* 341). Baldwin suggests that this is a tremendous exertion that few white Americans can achieve. For people who have not suffered – and here Baldwin directs his comments at white middle America – the experience of the blues cannot be translated. Echoing his interview with Nikki Giovanni, Baldwin wrote of how historically jazz had to be 'coded', but again insists that it 'has not been "de-coded"' since.[10] On the one hand, Baldwin writes of how the blues 'manages to make this [black] experience articulate' but he also suggests that it cannot always be heard by those who are outside of that experience.[11]

If Baldwin does not stake the claim that you need to be black to hear the blues, then he is clear that the music comes out of suffering and of understanding that condition. Writing in what would become a familiar riff on the guarded innocence of white America, Baldwin states that:

> There is something monstrous about never having been hurt . . . never having lost anything, never having gained anything because life is beautiful. . . . America is something like that. The failure on our part to accept the reality of pain, of anguish, of ambiguity, of death has turned us into a very peculiar and sometimes monstrous people.[12]

As we will see in relation to Baldwin's play, *The Amen Corner*, this failure to accept pain and suffering is not an exclusively white condition. If the above passage suggests that white Americans are cut off from experiences of suffering, he also explores the ways in which the black church stifles the transformation of pain. As I trace in Baldwin's writing on the blues, jazz and gospel music, suffering can be mediated, shared and transformed by the power of music. Starting with *Another Country* and his characterization of siblings Rufus and Ida, I turn to a discussion of Baldwin's play, *The Amen Corner*, his short story 'Sonny's Blues', and his final novel, *Just Above My Head*. Music for Baldwin is subversive and political but also something transformative: in Baldwin's writing music is often described in the language of spiritual awareness to the extent that at times it becomes, as I suggested in the previous chapter, the bedrock for a new kind of religious expression.

ANOTHER COUNTRY

Published in 1962, *Another Country*, catapulted Baldwin into the public eye. Though largely pilloried by New York critics, the novel was a huge bestseller and Baldwin became something of a celebrity. Set in New York, *Another Country* focuses on five characters whose lives interconnect and diverge, pulled together (and apart) by their gender, race, sexuality and class. As I discussed in Chapter 3, the novel is notable for its bold discussion of sex, both homosexual and interracial, but here I want to focus on Baldwin's engagement with music, in particular the jazz and blues. Two of the central characters are musicians: Rufus Scott, a young African American is a jazz drummer who throws himself off George Washington Bridge early in the novel and his sister, Ida, a singer whose story is also central to the novel.

Recollecting his vision of Manhattan in *Another Country*, Baldwin referred to it as 'the most unmerciful city in the Western world'.[13] *Another Country* plagues the reader with a myriad of stifling and haunting images of the city. This is a malevolent and encroaching New York, full of 'brutal sounds'; a menacing city that 'stared unsympathetically', casting shadows over unwelcoming doorways, a city where 'danger and horror [are] barely sleeping beneath the rough, gregarious surface' (*AC* 26, 36, 227). And, like Eliot's narrator in *The Waste Land*, who 'had not thought death had undone so many', the city is (un) peopled with 'dead eyes', a world already 'full of dead folks' (*AC* 49, 124).[14]

Baldwin's characters are thrust into this merciless urban metropolis, marooned on the island of Manhattan and disconnected from those around them. Music in this novel appears to at least offer some kind of solace, a way to make sense of this senseless world and to drown out 'the brutal sounds of the city' (*AC* 26). Love, but only its commodified form, is in the air: '*love me*' calls out from the radio, and 'long, syncopated synthetic laments for love' spew out of the jukebox until they are drowned out by commercials (*AC* 114, 79). The young saxophonist whose horn screams '*Do you love me? Do you love me? Do you love me?*' cannot offer love, but implores the listener indirectly through his savage horn (*AC* 18).

As Rufus listens to the young jazz musician he understands what his music is communicating: that he 'had received the blow from which he would never recover', that his horn tells the brutal tale of his damaged life (*AC* 18). Jazz, Baldwin suggests, is not only a sound for hip white cats to hang out to, but an existential cry: the music is not there to be enjoyed, rather it is something that confronts the listener. The music that Rufus hears in the jazz bar, Baldwin writes, 'was being hurled at the crowd like a malediction' (*AC* 14–15). It is the hard-bop murderous shout of Charlie Parker's horn, screaming out in music what cannot be told in words. Baldwin suggests that listening to the music is both a personal and a communal experience. The musicians 'blew what everyone had heard before'; Rufus gets the pain behind the saxophonist and the music, which, like an edgy Proustian Madeleine, sends him back to a past from which he thought he had escaped, for 'the beat of Harlem, which was simply the beat of his own heart' (*AC* 16–17).

Rufus cannot make sense of his past or present and ends his life by jumping off George Washington Bridge. As he waits for his subway train, a journey that will lead him to his suicide, Rufus realizes that 'we ain't never going to make it. We been fucked for fair', echoing the tormented saxophonist who 'had received a blow from which he would never recover' (*AC* 92, 18). But although Rufus is a musician, Baldwin does not allow him to articulate his grief, like the saxophonist, through music. Rufus becomes like Peter in Baldwin's short story 'Previous Condition', who cannot communicate what is happening to him: 'how can I explain to you what it feels like to be black when I don't understand it?' (*GTMTM* 92). In Rufus's case, his inability to communicate his situation is brutally played out at the moment of his death by the glimmer of car lights that 'seemed to be writing an endless message, writing with awful speed in a fine, unreadable script' (*AC* 93). It is only in the act of suicide, hurling himself into the abyss, that Rufus can communicate his depravity.

Before Rufus dies he listens to a recording of Bessie Smith singing 'Backwater Blues' with Vivaldo and Baldwin intersperses the lyrics into the two friends' dialogue. As Rufus listens to the voice of Bessie Smith he 'began to hear in the severely understated monotony of this blues, something which spoke to his troubled mind' (*AC* 57). This scene – and Baldwin's further use of female blues singers – is a crucial episode of the novel. Unlike the hard sound of the jazz musicians which communicates only pain and disinters buried memories, Baldwin suggests that Rufus begins to make sense of Bessie Smith's song. As Smith sings, Rufus 'wonders how others had moved beyond the emptiness and horror which faced him now' (*AC* 57). Though it is too late for Rufus, Baldwin suggests that Smith's lyrics and accompanying music, can *articulate* an experience that his protagonist can hear, providing narrative in an otherwise inchoate world.

As the friends talk, Vivaldo turns over the record and they listen to 'Empty Bed Blues', a moment that marks a shift in their conversation and speaks for the unarticulated erotic tension between the men. This moment is connected and reinforced much later in the novel when Eric, a bisexual actor, also listens to Bessie Smith.[15] Though Eric is white, Smith's voice 'hurled him, with violence, into the hot centre of his past', in part, Baldwin suggests, because of his Southern upbringing, but also on account of his bisexuality (*AC* 230). Baldwin intersperses the scene with haunting fragments of Smith's song that activate Eric's memory, one that 'could not really be recollected because it had become a part of him' (*AC* 235). As Eric listens to Smith, Rufus appears before him, a haunting disembodied image that echoes the disembodied, haunting sound of Smith singing through the phonograph.

In 'The Uses of the Blues' Baldwin suggests the ways in which Bessie Smith articulates an experienced history of pain and suffering. In the same essay, he also draws on Billie Holiday, a figure that Ida is loosely based upon. Not only are there biographical similarities (prostitution, relationship with white managers) but Ida reminds one listener 'of the young Billie Holiday' (*AC* 351).[16] Importantly, unlike the other main characters, Ida is not given a narrative voice, as if reminding Baldwin's white liberal readership that reading (or hearing) does not necessarily lead to understanding. Ida is repeatedly described as unknowable: she looks at Cass, 'unreadably', just as she later tells Cass, a patrician white woman, that 'there's no way in the world for you to know what Rufus went through . . .' (*AC* 126, 344).

If Ida is not accorded a narrative voice, then Baldwin suggests that her singing can speak about her experience, something that does not depend on the quality of her voice but her ability to express something that cannot be spoken. 'She was not a singer yet', Eric realizes, but has a 'quality [that] involves a sense of self so profound and so powerful that it does not so much leap barriers as reduce them to atoms' (*AC* 250). A little later in the novel, Baldwin also suggests that for Ida to become a great performer, 'she would have to . . . expose her audience . . . to her private fears and pain' (*AC* 253). And yet the paradox, as Baldwin also writes in a description of Ida's singing, is that 'this awful sense is private, unknowable, not to be articulated' (*AC* 250).

Baldwin's writing on Ida and on Smith and Holiday suggests not only that their singing is informed by their experiences of suffering, but that it is precisely such pain that defines their performances. Moreover, Baldwin is only too aware of the ways in which black females singers had to suffer in order to achieve success. Ida sleeps with Ellis, a wealthy white manager, in order to make it, but at some considerable cost. After one performance, when her affair has been found out, one of her accompanying musicians, a black male, ostracizes her from the musical community: 'You black white man's whore,' the bass player tells Ida, 'don't you never let me catch you on Seventh Avenue . . . I'll tear your little pussy *up*' (*AC* 415). Ida, though, has no other place to go: unlike many black female singers (most famously Mahalia Jackson and Aretha Franklin), Ida has no connections to a church community. And yet, as Baldwin hints during one exchange with Vivaldo, 'Nothing ever goes away'. 'I haven't thought of church or any of that stuff for years', Ida tells her lover, 'But it's still there' (*AC* 148). As I explore in the following sections, music remained an integral source for Baldwin's writing just as religion, too, clearly never goes away.

MUSIC AND THE CHURCH

Much of Baldwin's most impassioned writing about the church in his non-fiction comes from his excitement at the drama of the services, and in particular the power of the music. In *The Fire Next Time*, Baldwin recalls how

> The church was very exciting. It took a long time for me to disengage myself from this excitement . . . There is no music like that music, no drama like the drama of the saints rejoicing, the sinners moaning, the tambourines racing, and all those voices coming together and crying holy unto the Lord.   (CE 306)

In *Go Tell it on the Mountain*, too, the music is described as the driving force of the religious experience, a sound that 'swept on again, like fire, or flood, or judgment' (*GTM* 16). Although Baldwin recalled how, as a young preacher, he would 'improvise from the texts, like a jazz musician improvises from a theme', he was only too aware of the ways in which his Pentecostal church distinguished between 'religious' music and what Gabriel in *Go Tell it* refers to 'another music, infernal, which glorified lust and held righteousness up to scorn' (*CWJB* 234; *GTM* 158).

As I discussed in the introduction, as a teenager Baldwin had been encouraged by Beauford Delaney to listen to blues singers such as Ma Rainey and Bessie Smith – and crucially not to distinguish between 'religious' and 'non-religious' music. As Baldwin would suggest later in 'The Uses of the Blues', Ray Charles, though initially criticized by many in the church for his blend of gospel and blues, 'makes of a genuinely religious confession something triumphant and liberating' in his music.[17] For Baldwin, as he explores in his play, *The Amen Corner*, a work set in the church and dedicated to 'Nina [Simone], Ray [Charles], Miles [Davis], Bird [Charlie Parker]', the pain, love and anguish in the music of such artists is not far removed from the fundamental tenets of the church. As I examine through a reading of *The Amen Corner* and then *Just Above My Head*, music in Baldwin's work often has a salvific quality.

The Amen Corner, first performed at Howard University in 1955 (but not published until 1968) focuses on Sister Margaret, a Pentecostal minister in Harlem and her relationship to her son, David, and her estranged husband, Luke. Over the course of the play the audience learns that Margaret had lost her second child, finding solace (or refuge) in the church. As she entered the church, however, she also turned away from her jazz-playing husband, Luke, choosing the life of a minister over a loving sexual relationship. Baldwin's play picks up some familiar themes from his first novel, *Go Tell it on the Mountain* – the setting of the Harlem church, the relationship between fathers and sons – but he develops the idea of blues music and the way that the blues musician can teach others about suffering.

In *Go Tell it* there is a brief but telling scene where Gabriel is introduced to John Grimes for the first time. As the baby is presented to his future stepfather, he turns, not to Gabriel, but to the source of the gramophone playing a blues record down the hall (*GTM* 212–13). In *The Amen Corner*, Margaret, like Gabriel, forbids her son David to play blues records. 'The way that box is going, you wouldn't of hear the Holy *Ghost* come in', Margaret says about Luke's old record playing in her son's bedroom. 'Turn it off! Turn it off!' (*TAC* 88). And yet, as Baldwin suggests through David, a budding but clandestine jazz musician, there is little to separate the music heard in the church and the jazz played downtown in bars. 'Standing outside of the church', Zora Neale Hurston wrote about a jazz pianist in Jacksonville who played for sanctified church services and at parties, 'it is difficult to determine which kind of engagement he is filling at the moment'.[18] Echoing Hurston's observation, David tells Luke that he knows that the men who come back to the church aren't there for the Holy Ghost (as his mother believes) but to hear him play the piano (*TAC* 70).

If Baldwin suggests that music can be transformative, even religious – and that this can occur in a jazz bar and not just in a church – he also suggests through his iconoclastic character, Luke, that spirituality need not be restricted to the church. Luke, dying of tuberculosis, implores his son not 'to get away from the things that hurt you', echoing Baldwin's criticism of America's inability to confront pain and suffering (*TAC* 69). According to Luke, 'You got to learn to live with those things – and – use them', and indeed his music and understanding of suffering and love transform Margaret (*TAC* 69). At the end of the play, Luke dies and Margaret, extemporizing her sermon like a jazz musician, leaves the church, finally understanding what Baldwin wrote much later about the blues: that 'the acceptance of this anguish one finds in the blues, and the expression of it, creates also, however odd this may sound, a kind of joy'.[19]

'SONNY'S BLUES'

The relationship between suffering and religion is brought to the fore in Baldwin's most famous short story, 'Sonny's Blues', first published in 1957 and set in New York. The unnamed African American narrator works through his relationship with his estranged brother, Sonny, a jazz musician and heroin addict. When Sonny is arrested for possession of narcotics, the narrator, a conservative teacher, at first refuses to support his brother until he digs deep into his own experiences of suffering. Both moments of revelation or transformation occur while listening to music. Two thirds of the way through the story, the narrator pauses to watch a revival, transfixed, though he has seen many in Harlem, by the three black women and man performing on the street. The narrator is aware that the singers, who are collecting money for their singing, may not be particularly holy but he, along with the crowd of spectators, is struck by what he hears: 'As the singing filled the air the watching, listening faces underwent a change, the eyes focusing on something within; the music seemed to soothe a poison out of them' (*GTMTM* 130–1). Baldwin suggests that the music, at once a personal and collective experience, acts as a conduit or catalyst for something akin to religious awakening. Leaving the assembled crowd, the narrator notices that his brother, Sonny, has also been listening, further suggesting the ways in which music enables and forges connections between people. More immediately, the music becomes a way for Sonny and the narrator to reconnect since the narrator knows little about the kind of music that his brother digs (Charlie Parker). Their conversation is not about the music they have just heard or about the talents of the singer but about the experience behind it: 'it struck me all of a sudden', Sonny tells his brother, 'how much suffering she must have had to go through – to sing like that' (*GTMTM* 133–4).

The second description of music occurs after the revival when the narrator watches his brother play in a jazz bar in Greenwich Village. During the scene the narrator begins to understand music in the way that it expresses what cannot be talked about. 'All I know about music', the narrator says as he enters the bar, 'is that not many people ever really hear it' (*GTMTM* 139). As he watches his brother play, he begins to understand what the musician is able to communicate: 'the man who creates the music is hearing something else, is dealing with the roar rising from the void and imposing order on it as it hits the air'. In this description and elsewhere, Baldwin suggests that the musician is able to transform pain and absurdity, not into language like his own work as a writer, but 'another order, more terrible because it has no words, and triumphant, too, for that same reason' (*GTMTM* 139). As the narrator watches Sonny and his friends play, he begins to understand that 'they were keeping it new, at the risk of ruin, destruction, madness, and death, in order to find new ways to make us listen'. Crucially, Baldwin points out that what they played was not new itself, just as the force behind – the pain, suffering, anguish and joy – has been told and retold thousands of times: 'while the tale of how we suffer, and how we are delighted, and how we may triumph is never new, it always must be heard' (*GTMTM* 141). Baldwin suggests here that the task of musicians is to make these old stories sound new in order that we keep hearing them.

JUST ABOVE MY HEAD

Baldwin's last (and longest) novel, *Just Above My Head* was published in 1979 to mixed reviews. The tale focuses on the life and times of Arthur Montana, a gospel singer who later finds fame as the Soul Emperor. Two years after Arthur's death, his brother, Hall narrates his story. The novel, which switches from the mid-1940s to the mid-1970s has a large ensemble of characters who journey from Harlem to the South, Paris, London, Abidjan and San Francisco.

As in many of Baldwin's fictional works, the central protagonist in *Just Above My Head* is a musician. Here I want to focus on the significance of gospel music, a genre that sprung out of the church – and in particular the Pentecostal church – but also captured the popular public imagination. Unlike the blues, gospel has its roots in the church but the popularity of singers such as Mahalia Jackson and Boyd Rivers opened up the sound to audiences both secular and devout.[20] In *Just Above My Head*, there is a large roll-call of gospel, R&B singers and jazz musicians: Julia listens to Esther Phillips; Hall's son, Tony, is a fan of James Brown and later plays Billy Preston, and there are references to Dinah Shore, Mahalia Jackson, Ella Fitzgerald and the gospel maestro James Cleveland. It is gospel music that underscores the form and content of *Just Above My Head*. For James Campbell, Baldwin did not belong to one or other church but his life was nonetheless 'religious'; 'His scripture was the old black gospel music', a theory that is in part corroborated by Ernest Champion's account of Baldwin in the 1970s.[21] At Bowling Green University in the 1970s, Champion recalls both how Baldwin terrified his students by his blasphemous dismissal of God, but also how on one occasion, he broke down whilst hearing a gospel choir, unable to remain in the room. '[T]hey are singing my life', Baldwin told Champion, '[t]hat is where it all began'.[22]

Indeed Baldwin deploys music to invoke and make sense of the cultural, political and historical moments that his last novel maps out. In one of the few contemporary reviews that discussed Baldwin's use of music in *Just Above My Head*, James Campbell noted both how music was the 'second voice' of the narrator, Hall, but also that it made sense of the characters and the political and cultural terrain: 'Jazz, blues, gospel', Campbell wrote, 'constitute the vocabulary in which black history is written. It is a form of memory which outwits the white nightmare called history'.[23] Campbell astutely picks up the ways in which Baldwin uses music to speak for his characters' experiences, particularly in the brutal American South. As a young singer, Arthur travels with friends to sing in the South and his close friend, Peanut, disappears, kidnapped by white racists. Later Arthur performs a Civil Rights benefit in Florida but Baldwin suggests less that music has the power to transform racial politics, but rather that gospel articulates the unspeakable acts, what he describes in reference to the South as how 'no one wants to hear, now, what they did not dare to face then' (*JAMH* 410). For Hall, the novel's narrator, the quartet's music 'is black' because it come out of a particular experience of alienation and suffering (*JAMH* 304). Baldwin again suggests that black music does not refer to the lyrics but to the pain, triumph and love of a personal and yet collective experience: 'Niggers can sing gospel as no other people can because they're aren't singing the gospel . . . When a nigger quotes the Gospel, he is not quoting: he is telling you what happened to him today' (*JAMH* 113). Or, as he writes toward the end of the novel, 'Our history is each other . . . Perhaps that is what the gospel singer is singing' (*JAMH* 512).

If Baldwin suggests that gospel music is a mode of storytelling, a way of singing the histories of black America, then he also employs it to suggest new ways of forging relationships and nurturing love from outside of the church. In *Just Above My Head* Baldwin explores the relationship between gospel and the church. Arthur, the subject of the book, is pointedly described as non-religious in the traditional sense: 'He had not claimed to be saved', Hall recollects, 'He had not been baptized' (*JAHM* 90). Early in the novel, Hall recalls how Arthur was treated badly by the church after he 'branched out from gospel', and Baldwin challenges the traditional boundaries between religious and non-religious music and practice. Baldwin repeatedly describes Arthur's singing in a language shot through with religious vocabulary: 'When you sing', Arthur states, 'You can't sing *outside* the song. You've got to *be* the song you sing. You've got to make a confession' (*JAMH* 55). When Arthur sings, the church is 'wherever it was, whatever it was', whether a football field, stadium or music hall (*JAMH* 24–5).

In his last novel, Baldwin suggests that spirituality can – and indeed must – be found outside of the church. In Hall's discussion of gospel music, he suggests that authentic religion, expressed through music, is not just a song of devotion but a challenge to God: 'Maybe all gospel songs begin out of blasphemy and presumption', Hall ponders, 'what the church would call blasphemy and presumption: out of entering God's suffering, and making it your own, out of entering your suffering and challenging God Almighty to have or to give or to withhold mercy' (*JAMH* 8). This discussion of gospel music is central to Baldwin's novel: the music is not just a pleasing sound, nor is it just a way of expressing shared histories but it is something raw, painful and transformative, as suggested by Arthur's insistence that a song must be a confession.

In his discussion of *Just Above My Head*, Robert Reid-Pharr discusses what he calls 'the undeniable magic of gospel'. For Reid-Pharr, gospel 'presupposes a personal relationship with one's god, a relationship uncannily similar to that between lovers'.[24] I want to conclude this chapter by suggesting that Baldwin uses music – a force that he described in his last interview as his 'salvation' – to stand in for or rewrite institutional religious practice. In a radical twist, Baldwin suggests not only that salvation is more likely to be found outside of the church but also that music, particularly gospel, enables and speaks for an authentic spirituality based, not on the scripture, but on loving sexual relationships. Therefore, in *Just Above My Head*, playing and listening to gospel music becomes a way to share and explore love and suffering that was unavailable to Rufus in *Another Country*.

By using the spiritual heritage of gospel music, Baldwin redefines the boundaries of the secular and the sacrilegious. In both his penultimate novel, *If Beale Street Could Talk* and *Just Above My Head*, Baldwin invokes gospel music to signal and define a sexual love that retains a spiritual purity. In *Beale Street*, Tish explicitly refers to the gospel song , 'Steal Away' as she and Fonny make love. By noting how 'I was in his hands, he called me by the thunder at my ear. I was in his hands: I was being changed', Tish signifies on the gospel song: 'My Lord, He calls me, He calls me by thunder / The trumpet sound within my soul' (*IBSCT* 95).[25] As Fonny and Tish start to climax, Baldwin describes it as '[a] singing began in me and his body became sacred – his buttocks, as they quivered and rose and fell . . . brought me to another place' (*IBSCT* 97). The language used to described sexual communion is charged with rhetoric associated with religious experience; not only is Fonny's body explicitly described as 'sacred', but Tish is taken to 'another place', harmonizing conceptions of religious and sexual ecstasy. As I explore in the following chapter, Baldwin's work challenges the boundaries between the sacred and secular, radically calling into question the divisions between body and flesh, word and the Word.

5

Baldwin and Religion

The question of Baldwin and religion is indeed, as David Leeming puts it, 'a naughty one'.[1] As I explore in this chapter and discussed in the introduction, Baldwin who grew up in a fiercely religious household, left the church at the age of seventeen to embark on a different journey. And yet to suggest that Baldwin simply swapped the pulpit for the pen is to overlook his continuing fascination and preoccupation with religion and spirituality. Baldwin was deeply critical of aspects of the church and yet his work is shot through with biblical imagery, theologically nuanced commentaries and reflections on spirituality. As he acknowledged in 'Autobiographical Notes', the opening piece in his first collection of essays, his prose was deeply indebted to the King James Bible and yet the church's influence was by no means merely aesthetic.

As a child Baldwin had attended various Baptist churches with his father, including the famous Abyssinian Baptist Church on 138th Street in Harlem, run by the notorious preacher and congressman, Adam Clayton Powell. At some point in his early teenage years, Baldwin accompanied friends to the church of Mother Rosa Horn, the Mount Calvary Assembly of the Pentecostal Faith of All Nations. Mother Horn was well known in Harlem for attracting hundreds of worshippers and for her claims of healing the sick and even raising people from the dead. Baldwin would later move to another church, the Fireside Pentecostal Assembly, where, at the age of fourteen, he became 'a Holy Roller Preacher'.[2]

Baldwin's brief encounter with Mother Horn's church is important for two particular reasons. The Harlem of his youth, Baldwin recalled, was a place where 'the wages of sin were visible everywhere'. As a young boy, vulnerable to sexual molestation, Baldwin felt 'one of the most depraved people on earth', causing him to flee to the safety of the church (*CE* 299, 297). Baldwin's early teenage years, as David Leeming notes, were a period in 'which he was to be nearly overwhelmed by sexuality, and, almost at the same moment, by religion'.[3] This connection between religion and sexuality is a crucial – if not central – dynamic in Baldwin's writing. In his recollection of joining Mother Horn's church, Baldwin is struck by the similarity between the church and the sexual depravity of the streets. Mother Horn's first question, '[w]hose little boy are you?' was, Baldwin wrote, the same question asked by pimps and racketeers. Moving to the church, Baldwin recalls was 'a spiritual seduction', not far removed from the sexual activity of the streets (*CE* 303). Even the moment of conversion, as David Leeming notes, led Baldwin 'to sense the sexual roots of the terrifying release he had experienced on the church floor as Mother Horn and the saints had labored over him'.[4]

Although Baldwin did not remain in Mother Horn's church for long, his introduction to Pentecostalism had a profound effect on his teenage years, and I would argue, on his views on the church and spirituality. Baldwin's move from his father's Baptist church to the storefronts of Pentecostalism represents a significant shift. Unlike mainstream Baptist churches, Pentecostalism was often viewed with suspicion and was dogged with rumours that its preachers were uneducated charlatans who set up make-shift churches in storefronts, often earning a substantial wage from donations. In contrast to the respectable and grandiose churches such as the Abyssinian Baptist Church on 138th Street, Pentecostal churches were often viewed as lower class places where the disreputable congregations sang and played music and spoke in tongues.

Although Pentecostalism in the United States has historically been met with what one theologian calls 'suspicion and disapprobation', for Zora Neale Hurston the Sanctified Church, formed at the turn of the twentieth century, was formed as a 'protest' against the emphasis on materiality and focus on money in middle-class churches.[5] For many writers, however, black American storefront churches are the butt of satirical writings where the preacher is on the make. In

Langston Hughes's play, *Tambourines for Glory* (1956), for example, Buddy exclaims that '[t]his church racket's got show business beat to hell', adding that 'some churches don't have sense enough to be crooked . . . and holiness don't make money'.[6] Despite the popular images of storefront churches, theologians such as Cheryl Sanders have stressed that early Pentecostal churches were in fact anti-materialistic. Echoing Hurston's claim that Pentecostalism was formed as a reaction to the middle-class churches, Sanders writes that the Holiness Movement 'came out of the mainline black denominational churches and sought the deeper life of entire sanctification and Spirit Baptism'.[7]

As I explore shortly, Baldwin was keenly aware of the contradictory aspects of Pentecostalism. On the one hand, he saw the church as a 'racket', suggesting the ways in which it exploited the largely working-class congregation. He was also deeply critical of the puritanical renunciation of the flesh, a theme he continued to write about. Yet there are moments of awe and wonder in Baldwin's work when it becomes clear that Pentecostalism had a profound effect on his writing and outlook, whether it is in the power of the music or his powerful descriptions of conversion. As late as 1985 in the introduction to *The Price of the Ticket* Baldwin wrote that 'Once I had left the pulpit, I had abandoned or betrayed my role in the community . . .' (*CE* 838).

BALDWIN'S ESSAYS ON RELIGION

Baldwin's vitriolic attacks on the church in his bestselling essay and book, *The Fire Next Time* in 1963, have led many readers and critics to conclude that he had become a secular writer. In fact, as Rolf Lunden has pointed out, his splenetic tirades against the church in *Fire* had tinged his earlier, more positive descriptions of Christianity. As Lunden notes, few if any critics interpreted *Go Tell it on the Mountain* as an indictment of Christianity or an ironic commentary until *The Fire Next Time*.[8] In what follows I want to explore Baldwin's views on the church in *The Fire Next Time* before going on to read his fictional descriptions of Christianity.

Baldwin's two essays which became *The Fire Next Time* became something of a turning point in writing of the Civil Rights movement and it's important to read his criticism of the church in this context. Baldwin's essay 'Down at the Cross' begins with his recollection of how, aged fourteen, he experienced 'a prolonged religious crisis', explaining that he 'discovered God, His saints and angels, and His blazing Hell' (*CE* 296). As Baldwin points out, for a young impoverished African American in Harlem, there weren't many options for survival. 'Some went on wine or whiskey or the needle', Baldwin recalls, while 'others, like me, fled into the church' (*CE* 299). As Baldwin's use of the word 'fled' suggests, the church was viewed as a place of safety, or a 'gimmick' as he referred to it in the same essay (*CE* 301). Despite Baldwin's scepticism, there are moments where he attests to the power of his experience, most strikingly in a description of his conversion, described by the author as 'the strangest sensation I have ever had in my life' (*CE* 304). In a remarkable description Baldwin captures the awe and terror of this transformative moment. Unexpectedly, Baldwin finds himself on his back with the saints above him filled with an anguish that 'cannot be described'. When he attempts to relive that moment, Baldwin couches it in apocalyptic terms where the spirit 'moved in me like one of those floods that devastate counties, tearing everything down, tearing children from their parents and lovers from each other, and making everything an unrecognizable waste' (*CE* 304).

Crucially, Baldwin then rhetorically brings the reader down to earth as he reflects on his experience. 'But God – and I felt this even then, so long ago, on that tremendous floor, unwillingly – is white'. At the very moment that he is 'saved', Baldwin has another epiphany, suggesting that his political consciousness was born: 'And if His love was so great, and if He loved all His children, why were we, the blacks, cast down so far? Why?' (*CE* 304–5). This experience of conversion, I would suggest, had a profound effect on Baldwin's writing. The conversion is described without irony and there is an acknowledgement of the power of the Holy Spirit. The church, Baldwin writes, was a place that he continued to find 'exciting', adding that 'It took a long time for me to disengage myself from this excitement, and on the blindest, most visceral level, I never really have, and never will' (*CE* 306). Despite his acknowledgement that his own experience was powerful and inexplicable, Baldwin recalls that he could not disentangle this from the hypocrisy of the church, whether black or white.

Baldwin maintains that African Americans have been 'taught really to despise themselves from the moment their eyes open on the world', and the white church has done nothing to counter this (*CE* 302). The Bible, Baldwin notes, was written by white men and that 'according to many Christians, I was a descendant of Ham, who had been cursed, and that I was therefore predestined to be a slave' (*CE* 307). Here Baldwin's view that the white church justified slavery anticipates the work of African American theologians such as James Cone, who have forcefully argued that 'the white church's involvement in slavery and racism in America simply cannot be overstated'.[9] Like Cone, Baldwin rails against Christianity's complicity in the mechanisms of slavery and colonialism, arguing vehemently that '[t]he spreading of the Gospel . . . was an absolutely indispensable justification for the planting of the flag' (*CE* 313). For Baldwin, armed with the knowledge of (white) Christianity's dubious history, his position as a minister became increasingly problematic. '[I]t began to take all the strength I had not to stammer, not to curse', Baldwin recalled, 'not to tell them [the congregation] to throw away their Bibles and get off their knees and go home and organize, for example, a rent strike' (*CE* 309).

For Baldwin, the black church, though at least offering a place of refuge for people like his father (or indeed for the teenage Jimmy), was not only a place devoid of love but it was also 'a mask for hatred and self-hatred and despair' (*CE* 309). Believing that the edict 'love everybody' meant *everybody*, Baldwin quickly found that this did not apply to white people, leading the young minister to question the reason for his own salvation. In the end for Baldwin, it comes down to love – a crucial if often misunderstood theme in the author's work: 'If the concept of God has any validity or any use', Baldwin writes, 'it can only be to make us larger, freer, and more loving. If God cannot do this, then it is time we get rid of Him' (*CE* 314).

RELIGION IN BALDWIN'S FICTION

I want to turn now to explore Baldwin's descriptions of the church and spirituality in his fiction, focusing on his first novel, *Go Tell it on Mountain*, his play *The Amen Corner* and a short story from his collection *Going to Meet the Man*. As my readings suggest, I'm not convinced that Baldwin 'got rid' of his preoccupation with spirituality – even if he became increasingly critical of the church as an institution. I also want to make it clear that there are numerous other works in Baldwin's *oeuvre* that either use biblical imagery or are concerned with theological issues. In his first significant essay, for example, 'Everybody's Protest Novel', Baldwin is drawn to what he sees as the 'theological terror', of *Uncle Tom's Cabin* and most – if not all – of his works, whether fiction or non-fiction draw on religious imagery, such as the biblical references to Jonathan and David in *Giovanni's Room* (*CE* 14).

Go Tell it on the Mountain

Looking back on the completion of his first novel, Baldwin recalled that he 'had come through something', as he finally finished the project that had taken him ten years to complete.[10] *Go Tell it on the Mountain*, was Baldwin recalled, an attempt 'to re-create the life that I had first known as a child and from which I had spent so many years in flight' (*CE* 138). Set in Harlem during the 1930s, *Go Tell it on the Mountain* takes place on the fourteenth birthday of John Grimes, an illegitimate African American from Harlem. During the novel, Baldwin explores John's difficult relationship with his stepfather, Gabriel, a disciplinarian preacher, an experience that the author shared with his protagonist. During the course of the novel John experiences a burgeoning sexual awakening that coincides with his entrance into the church.

As Cheryl Sanders has remarked, Baldwin's recollection that he had 'come through something' suggests that the completion of *Go Tell it* was akin to the experience of religious conversion: an attempt, both to come to terms with, and to exorcize his sanctified past.[11] In the process of 'coming through', a phrase which draws on the protagonist's own tortuous salvation on the threshing floor, Baldwin attempted to lay his past to rest with an earlier draft titled 'Crying Holy' (one of the characteristic expressions of the Pentecostal worship experience), followed by three thematically similar short stories: 'In My Father's House', 'The Death of a Prophet', and 'Roy's Wound'.

Whilst the different versions of what would eventually become *Go Tell it on the Mountain* are characterized by a young protagonist's tortuous relationship with his stepfather, early readers of Baldwin's most substantial draft, 'Crying Holy', noted its explicit homoeroticism. The poet Harold Norse, a friend of Baldwin's from his Greenwich Village days, recalls that 'Crying Holy' was not only 'beautifully written', but '[i]t was the first time I had seen the subject of homosexuality in a contemporary novel'.[12] Similarly, Emile Capouya, a school friend of Baldwin's who had also read a similar draft, describes how the original story ended with John saying (in effect) 'I want a man'.[13] Baldwin, according to Norse, was pessimistic about getting his novel published: 'Who'd ever take it? . . . Who wants a novel about a black boy anyway, much less a queer one?'[14] Although Baldwin toned down the explicitly homosexual relationship between John and Elisha in *Go Tell it*, it remains as critics have begun to argue, 'deeply buried' within the narrative, a point that Baldwin acknowledged, noting that it 'is implicit in the boy's situation', and 'made almost explicit' in his tentative relationship with Elisha.[15]

As I noted in Chapter 3, critics such as Michael Cobb have started to pay attention to the 'complicated relations between queerness, blackness, and religious rhetoric' in Baldwin's work.[16] Cobb convincingly argues that the queerness of the story is there but deflected or sublimated, 'told, however indirectly and violently through a more recognizable drama of pain and violence: the drama of race'.[17] As Cobb suggests, Baldwin would have been unable to deal with blackness and queerness in 1953 and his first major works – novels and essays – deal with the subject of race, then sexuality – but not together. After *Go Tell it on the Mountain*, Baldwin would publish *Giovanni's Room*, a significant novel about homosexuality but one without any black characters. Again, Baldwin's first major essay on race, 'Everybody's Protest Novel', was followed in the same magazine by 'Preservation of Innocence', a bold examination of homosexuality that does not deal with race.

Contemporary reviewers of *Go Tell it on the Mountain*, however, failed to pick up on the homoeroticism of the novel. If the novel was described as excessive (often a euphemism for homosexual) this was because it drew too heavily on the rituals of the church. Baldwin's editors, for example, took exception to what they saw as the excessive religiosity of the novel. William Cole, whilst noting that the 'novel [is] rich and poetic', reported that '[s]ome of the long "Come to Jesus!" passages should be cut', a comment that Baldwin reprinted with indignation in the introduction to *The Amen Corner* (*TAC* 11). Similarly, although early reviewers of *Go Tell it* praised Baldwin's fluid style, describing it as 'essentially a religious novel' there was no mention of the novel's homoeroticism.[18]

I want to argue here that Baldwin's first novel is characterized by a series of powerful tensions that reverberate through the narrative: the awe of conversion and the anger at the hypocrisy of the church and the power of the spirit but a refusal to renounce, mortify or ignore the body. While I agree with Cobb's nuanced reading of *Go Tell it on the Mountain*, I suggest, through a reading of other works set in the church, that Baldwin is preoccupied with the tensions between sexual relationships and spirituality more generally, whether gay, straight or bisexual. And, most troubling of all for contemporary literary critics, Baldwin's work is shot through with examinations of love.

Baldwin's first novel is also a remarkable tale about loneliness told through the bulging eyes of the fourteen-year-old John Grimes. Bowed down with the expectation that he will become a preacher like his father, John Grimes is cut off from the pleasures of childhood. Even the simple joys of playing with a ball fill John with a feeling of guilt and retribution as the ball 'bounced as he jumped, like a bright omen above his head' (*GTM* 34). In John's fiercely religious world, the body is something to be ignored, repressed and even reviled. In the sermons that the young protagonist hears from Father James, John is constantly reminded that 'the Word was hard, that the way of holiness was a hard way' (*GTM* 18). In the Pentecostal Harlem community where John and his family worship, there is no room for deviation from the hard way of the Lord; as Sister McCandless points out: 'You is in the Word or you *ain't* – ain't no half-way with God' (*GTM* 68). Baldwin paints a picture of an isolated and claustrophobic community far removed from the bustle and cosmopolitan vitality usually associated with Harlem. In the Pentecostalist's eyes, the world outside of the church is 'Broadway', a place of sin 'where the unconquerable odour was of dust, and sweat, and urine, and home-made gin' (*GTM* 39).

In Baldwin's narrative, it becomes clear that such neat divisions (broad and narrow ways, the Word and flesh, sinner and saved) are not only damaging but – and this is crucial in his writing – they are fabrications which always threaten to break down. This is most explicit in the ways that his work explores the tensions between religion and sexuality. As John cleans the church, his thoughts turn from the abstractions of the Lord to the 'the odour of dust and sweat' that overwhelms his senses (*GTM* 57). Worship, Baldwin illustrates, requires the body as well as the spirit to participate: when 'praying or rejoicing, their bodies gave off an acrid, steamy smell, a marriage of the odours of dripping bodies and soaking, starched white linen', an earthy and sensual odour that is reminiscent of the smells of dust, sweat and gin found on Broadway (*GTM* 58).

Baldwin is at pains to point out the power of the body beneath the holy robes. When the pastor's nephew, Elisha, is 'saved', his most spiritual moment is marked, not by his spiritual re-birth, but by the physicality of his trembling body, as 'his thighs moved terribly against the cloth of his suit' (*GTM* 17). When Elisha is later publicly reprimanded for 'walking disorderly' with Ella Mae, Baldwin describes how her 'white robes now seemed to be the merest, thinnest covering for the nakedness of breasts and insistent thighs . . .' (*GTM* 19). During the church service, Baldwin suggests that sexual energy and desire is at times indistinguishable from religious ecstasy, illustrated by his description of Elisha on the piano: 'At one moment, head thrown back, eyes closed, sweat standing on his brow, he sat at the piano, singing and playing; and then . . . he stiffened and trembled, and cried out, *Jesus, Jesus, oh Lord Jesus!*' (*GTM* 16). Here the religious ecstasy that Elisha experiences is

81

infused with sexual energy, written in a language that closely mirrors Ida and Vivaldo's lovemaking in *Another Country*: 'he was aching in a way he had never ached before, was congested in a new way . . . *Come on come on come on come on. Come on!*' (*AC* 177–8).

Baldwin does not only suggest that sexual and religious ecstasy is similar but, in a more radical move, that spirituality is fuelled by sexual desire. In the description of Elisha, for example, his moaning fills the church and infects the congregation so that 'the rhythm of all the others quickened to match Elisha's rhythm', climaxing with 'a great moaning [that] filled the church'. As if defying the reader not to link the sexual with the holy, the next line reads: '[t]here was sin among them' (*GTM* 17). Similarly, during flashbacks to Gabriel's life as a young married preacher in the South, Baldwin suggests that the power of his sermon – one that is remembered for years to come – is fuelled, not by his religious fervour, but by sexual tension. As Gabriel preaches, trying to stave off his desire for Esther, his sermon, directed at his object of desire, sweeps through the congregation and rocks the church. When he finally succumbs to his desire, Gabriel feels the 'mystery' and 'passion' in her body, a description of sex couched in religious rhetoric (*GTM* 145).

Gabriel's severity – even cruelty – in later years, Baldwin suggests, stems from his renunciation of the body, compounded by the guilty memory of his adultery. As Clarence Hardy has argued, Baldwin rejected white Christianity's demonizing of the black body ('the legend [of how] the black body itself is depicted as the creation of the devil done against "the commands of God"') but also lambasted the black church's inability or unwillingness to counter a deeply embedded black self-loathing.[19] In *Go Tell it*, Baldwin explores the latter theme through an episode where John sees his father's nakedness, linking this to the curse of Ham. Baldwin links the account in Genesis – where Noah curses Ham's son, Canaan, for seeing Ham naked – to the enslavement of the Canaanites, a story often associated with black American slavery. Throughout the novel John is troubled by his burgeoning sexual desire and the fear of eternal damnation, what Baldwin describes in his short story 'The Outing', as 'the sordid persistence of the flesh' (*GTMTM* 41). As John imagines the body of a woman on the ceiling of his bedroom, this momentary image of sexual desire is quickly usurped by fear, dreaming that he has awoken on Judgement Day 'left, with his sinful body, to be bound in hell a thousand years' (*GTM* 20).

As I explored in Chapter 3, in both *Go Tell it* and 'The Outing', Baldwin suggests that his protagonists are able to find solace and comfort through love for other boys but the queerness of such desire is muted, whispered rather than fully articulated. Baldwin writes of John, 'In the school lavatory, alone, thinking of the boys, older, bigger, braver, who made bets with each other as to whose urine could arch higher, he had watched in himself a transformation of which he would never dare to speak' (*GTM* 20). In a later passage, echoing the 'unspeakable' thoughts that he has as he thinks of other boys, John literally reflects on his sin, as he 'stared at his face as though it were . . . the face of a stranger, a stranger who held secrets that John could never know' (*GTM* 30).

The references to queer desire are important, illustrating, as Cobb writes, the ways in which 'religious language is a strong language that simultaneously hides *and* articulates the queer within the more 'normal' and recognizable narratives of racial violence, pleasure . . .'.[20] In Baldwin's descriptions of John and Elisha in *Go Tell it* and David and Johnnie in 'The Outing', sexual desire, as I explored in Chapter 3, is inextricably linked to religious transformation. Crucially, both of these accounts are rendered in a language that is religious in its intensity and vocabulary. In other words, it is not simply that the four boys find love or desire instead of spirituality, but that they cross the river of spiritual belief with the help of another person. As Baldwin would later describe in *Nothing Personal*, 'a human being could only be saved by another human being' (*PT* 388–9). In 'The Outing', Baldwin makes this even more explicit as Johnnie feels the awful terror of the Lord. As Johnnie feels overwhelmed by the timeless cacophony of wailing and fire, at the very moment when he seems to give in to the Lord, 'Johnnie felt suddenly, not the presence of the Lord, but the presence of David; which seemed to reach out to him, hand reaching out to hand in the fury of flood-time, to drag him to the bottom of the water or to carry him safe to shore' (*GTMTM*

47). Rather than turning to God, Johnnie is 'saved' by the love and desire of David; he feels, 'such a depth of love, such nameless and terrible joy and pain, that he might have fallen, in the face of that company, weeping at David's feet' (*GTMTM* 48). As Baldwin's near apocalyptic descriptions of conversion suggest, he is not concerned with categories that divide, but in moments that tear these walls asunder. Baldwin challenges the divisions between the body and the flesh, or indeed the oppositions of love/desire and spirituality. In Baldwin's writing, he frequently suggests that love *is* spirituality.

It would be hard to deny that Baldwin became increasingly critical of the black and white church over his career. In his later fiction there are few positive descriptions of characters who are 'saved'. Fonny's mother in *If Beale Street Could Talk* is described as 'a Sanctified woman, who didn't smile much', foregrounding the harsh piety of Julia, the child preacher in *Just Above My Head* (*IBSCT* 21). In *Tell Me How Long the Train's Been Gone*, Baldwin suggests that religion can stifle – even efface – the sensual vitality that the author celebrates in his characters, like Caleb who finds the Lord but 'did not want to be Caleb any more' (*TMHL* 334). Baldwin sets out his distinctions between religion and love most clearly in the introduction to *The Amen Corner* where he explains the actions of his protagonist, Margaret. 'Her need for human affirmation, and also her vengeance', Baldwin writes 'expresses itself in her merciless piety'. Baldwin does not deny that her love is real but asserts that it has been soured by 'an absolutely justifiable terror', so that she loses her 'old self'. Margaret, however, ultimately triumphs, gaining, Baldwin writes, 'the keys to the kingdom'. In unequivocal language, Baldwin writes that 'The kingdom is love, and love is selfless, although only the self can lead one there. She gains herself' (*TAM* 14).

Baldwin's work suggests, not that connections between people *replace* religion, but that love between people, whether sexual or spiritual, is itself a religious experience. This is illustrated by his many characters who are outside of the church but who nonetheless have spiritual authority, including Frank in *The Amen Corner* and Arthur in *Just Above My Head*. For Baldwin, as he wrote in *Tell Me How Long the Train's Been*

Gone, the most important act is 'the touch of another: no matter how transient, at no matter what price' (*TMHL* 270). Despite his reputation as a fiery polemicist and embittered prose writer, Baldwin's work is preoccupied with explorations of love, one of the most prominent themes in his writing but one which critics have largely ignored. First, it is important not to confuse Baldwin's emphasis on love with sentimentality, a feeling that he explicitly warns against.[21] Second, his definition of love is explicitly active and political. Echoing Cornel West's warning that a 'love ethic has nothing to do with sentimental feelings or tribal connections', and Martin Luther King's insistence that 'love is not to be confused with some sentimental outpouring', Baldwin points out that, by focusing on love, he does not 'mean anything passive' but rather 'something active, something more like a fire ... something which can change you ... I mean a passionate belief, a passionate knowledge of what a human being can do ...' (*CWJB* 48).[22] Like King who spoke of love as 'a force', Baldwin wrote both that he conceived of God 'as a means of liberation', and also that '[l]ove is a battle, love is a war; love is a growing up' (*CE* 220).[23] Baldwin's insistence on the need for love has been misunderstood by critics as a panacea to the struggle for civil rights. His description in *The Fire Next Time* of the black-white relationship in America as like that of 'lovers' confounded critics who expected to hear the voice of Jeremiah. As Baldwin's explanations make clear, however, he understands love as something tough and transformative. Love, whether sexual or religious, is the fundamental tenet of his spiritual outlook. 'I'm not a believer in any sense that would make sense to any church', Baldwin stated in 1965, 'and any church would obviously throw me out. I believe – what do I believe? I believe in ... love' (*CWJB* 48).

Conclusion

As Carol Henderson has recently pointed out, there has been something of a 'renaissance' in Baldwin studies since the end of the 1990s.[1] In 1999 Dwight McBride edited a pioneering volume of essays, *James Baldwin Now*, which argued for the importance of viewing the late writer's work in its complexity, challenging earlier critical narratives that had viewed Baldwin as either black or gay, American or African American. McBride's collection was followed by D. Quentin Miller's wide ranging collection, *Re-Viewing James Baldwin: Things Not Seen* (2000). More recent works include Lynne Scott's *James Baldwin's Later Fiction: Witness to the Journey* (2002), a much needed rejoinder to the lazy critical orthodoxy that overlooks Baldwin's last three novels. Baldwin's influence on other African American writers is reflected in *James Baldwin and Toni Morrison: Comparative and Critical Essays*, edited by Lynn Scott and Lovalerie King (2006), a volume which sheds light on each writer, exploring how their works diverge and converge. In 2008 Magdalena Zaborowska's award-winning book, *James Baldwin's Turkish Decade: Erotics of Exile* broke new ground by exploring Baldwin's interrupted ten years in Turkey, urging the importance of seeing Baldwin outside of the familiar North American and European critical framework. That year, Herb Boyd's, *Baldwin's Harlem: A Biography of James Baldwin* mapped out his relationship to Harlem, the place of his childhood. Clarence Hardy's *James Baldwin's God: Sex, Hope and Crisis in Black Holiness Culture* (2009) provided a useful framework for understanding Baldwin's relationship to the Holiness church. Surprisingly, this is the first book devoted to a study of the writer's theological concerns. My own edited collection, *A*

Historical Guide to James Baldwin (2009) stresses the importance of viewing the author through the four decades he worked as a writer, exploring his religious, queer, transatlantic and political identities. Finally, a new volume of Baldwin's has appeared that includes book reviews and articles. *The Cross of Redemption: Uncollected Writings* (2010), edited by Randall Kenan, alongside *The Price of the Ticket: Collected Nonfiction, 1948–1985* (1985) and the 1998 Library of America, *Collected Essays*, shows the extent of Baldwin's output, with essays on topics ranging from black English, his Harlem youth, Shakespeare and on white liberalism.

The continuing interest in Baldwin's life and work illustrates the ways that his voice speaks across generations, nationalities and ethnicities. It suggests the ways that Baldwin's fiction and non-fiction remains relevant, especially thanks to the author's relentless examination of national identity, the pitfalls of liberalism, and his insistence on the complexities of modern life. Baldwin's impact on the twentieth century literary and political landscape was highlighted at his funeral at New York's Cathedral of St John the Divine on 8 December 1987 where writers including Toni Morrison, Maya Angelou, Amiri Baraka, and William Styron paid tribute to the author. Baldwin, Morrison stated, 'made American English honest', adding that he 'gave us undecorated truth'. It was Baldwin, Morrison continued, 'who gave us the courage to live life in an alien, hostile, all-white geography'.[2] Angelou recalled Baldwin as her friend and brother, extolling his capacity to love.[3] In a fiery eulogy, Baraka remembered Baldwin, not just as a writer, but 'a man, spirit, voice – old and black and terrible as that first ancestor'. Baldwin, Baraka reminded the congregation, was 'God's black revolutionary mouth', a 'civil rights leader' who, as much as Malcolm X and Dr King, 'helped shepherd and guide us toward black liberation'.[4] The tributes by Morrison, Angelou, Baraka, and Styron point to the diverse ways in which Baldwin's contributions to American literature have been assessed. For many readers and critics, Baldwin's voice has become synonymous with the literature of black rage and exasperation of the 1960s. Baldwin's repeated attacks on racism, as Morrison suggests, opened the literary floodgates for numerous African American writers, including Morrison herself. And yet as the political fervour of the 1960s and early 1970s diminished, Baldwin's work, as Styron covertly suggests, was greeted with a lukewarm critical reception. More often than not critics pointed to a fading craft that failed to deliver the power of works such as *The Fire Next Time*. As John Wideman noted shortly after Baldwin's death, there was a recalcitrant critical consensus that Baldwin 'lost his footing as an artist and simply became a propagandist'.[5] More recently critics have begun to break the silence surrounding Baldwin's sexuality, a point that I examined in my third chapter. As Emmanuel Nelson has rightly pointed out, the tributes by Morrison, Angelou, Baraka and Styron 'conveniently forget to mention Baldwin's struggle against sexual fascism and his central place in gay literature'.[6] The silence continued when Chinua Achebe, Michael Thelwell and John Wideman (amongst others) presented papers at the University of Massachusetts to honour and appraise Baldwin's life and work. Aside from Thelwell's murmur that Baldwin spoke about sex and race 'openly and honestly', there was no examination of Baldwin's contribution or struggle as a queer writer.[7] And yet since Nelson's claims in 1992, numerous critics have given voice to Baldwin's depictions of masculinity, bisexuality and homosexuality. In fact, according to Dwight McBride, cultural studies has finally enabled us to see Baldwin in his entirety, 'locating him not as exclusively gay, black, expatriate, activist, or the like but as an intricately negotiated amalgam of all those things'.[8]

Since McBride's introduction to his volume of essays, there have been a number of important critical inroads into Baldwin's work. At the same time, there are still a number of under-researched areas, which illustrate the sheer volume and scope of the writer's work. Though there have been some pioneering critical studies on Baldwin's life and work, the scholarship is by no means exhausted. No single authored volume yet examines all six of Baldwin's novels, and, despite Scott's discussion of the writer's last three novels, there is still little sustained criticism on *Tell Me How Long the Train's Been Gone*, *If Beale Street Could Talk* and *Just Above My Head*. It is now over twenty five years since Trudier Harris's ground breaking study, *Black Women in the Fiction of James Baldwin* (1985) and there is still little criticism on Baldwin's characterization of white women, such as Leona in *Another Country* or Hella in *Giovanni's Room*. Aside from Quentin Miller's essay in his edited volume, critics have shied away from analyses of Baldwin's two volumes of poetry and there is scant criticism on the writer's interest in visual media, such as his photo-text collaboration, *Nothing Personal* or his book on film, *The Devil Finds Work*. There is little work on Baldwin as a public speaker, although a quick search on the internet reveals scores of his electric performances. There is extended footage of Baldwin in the recently re-released film, *Baldwin's Nigger* (1969), where he talks for over twenty minutes at London's West Indian Centre, accompanied by the comedian Dick Gregory. There is work to be done on Dick Fontaine's 1982 documentary, *I Heard it Through the Grapevine*, which features Baldwin and his brother, David, as well as on Stan Lathan's 1984 film adaptation of *Go Tell it on the Mountain*. Finally, though the biographies by Leeming and Campbell have added much to an understanding of Baldwin's life and work, there is no single biography that compares in depth and length to the exhaustive works on other African American authors such as Ralph Ellison, Langston Hughes and W. E. B. Du Bois.[9]

The research yet to be done on Baldwin's work (a list, no doubt that will keep growing) is both testament to the pioneering scholarship that has already been done and a reminder of the enormous legacy of the writer's life and work where there are still exciting unchartered critical territories to be mapped and explored. It is tempting to think about what Baldwin would have made of his increasingly secure critical legacy; the maverick from Harlem, with no formal education beyond the age of seventeen; the unpredictable writer and fiery personality who not only courted readers but demanded to be heard. One wonders, too, what Baldwin would make of the first black president in American history. In his 1965 essay, 'American Dream and the American Negro', he recalls the 'laughter and bitterness and scorn' in Harlem which greeted Robert Kennedy's statement that there could be a black US president in the next forty years (*CE* 718). What would Baldwin have made of the invasion of Iraq and Afghanistan and 9/11? By the early 1970s Baldwin connected American involvement in Vietnam to the country's thirst for global imperialism. In *No Name* he is adamant that black Americans had no business in Vietnam, 'aiding the slave master to enslave yet more millions of dark people' (*CE* 364). One can speculate what Baldwin would have made of the global recession, brought on by the greed of corporations, something he was attuned to as early as 1963 in his essay 'A Talk to Teachers'. Here Baldwin shows his awareness of how ghettos are constructed and maintained, pulling no punches when he writes that 'black men were brought here as a source of cheap labor. They were indispensable to the economy' (*CE* 681). Again, as early as 1962, in his essay 'Color', Baldwin anticipated later discussions about 'colour blindness' and 'post-racial America' in his sharp analysis where he muses that 'to be colored means that one has been caught in some utterly unbelievable cosmic joke, a joke so hideous and in such bad taste that it defeats all categories and definitions' (*CE* 673). 'White people', Baldwin wrote in the introduction to *The Price of the Ticket*, 'are not white: part of the price of the white ticket is to delude themselves into believing that they are' (*CE* 835).

Baldwin's legacy will become increasingly secure as critics and readers recognize the ways in which he helped shape twentieth century American literature. Not only was he an exquisite stylist gifted with original insight, but his work is structured around enduring themes of love, anguish, hope, isolation and spirituality. Baldwin's work is forward looking, even prophetic, but also aware of the need to look, not only back, but inwards. As Baldwin wrote in the introduction to *The Price of the Ticket*, 'Go back to where you started, or as far back as you can, examine all of it, travel your road again and the truth about. Sing or shout or testify or keep it to yourself: but *know whence you came*' (*PT* xix).

Notes

INTRODUCTION. SITUATING JAMES BALDWIN

1. The two most comprehensive biographies of Baldwin are: James Campbell, *Talking at the Gates: A Life of James Baldwin* (London: Faber, 1991) and David Leeming, *James Baldwin: A Biography* (New York: Alfred A. Knopf, 1994). For an earlier account based mainly on interviews, see Fern Marja Eckman, *The Furious Passage of James Baldwin* (New York: M. Evans & Co, 1966). For an entertaining biography of Baldwin, see W. J. Weatherby, *James Baldwin: Artist on Fire, A Portrait* (London: Michael Joseph, 1990).
2. David Leeming, *Amazing Grace: A Life of Beauford Delaney* (New York and Oxford: Oxford University Press, 1998), xiii.
3. Leeming, *James Baldwin: A Biography*, 33.
4. 'Nation: The Root of the Negro Problem', *Time* (17 May 1964), http://www.time.com/time/magazine/article/0,9171,830 326,00.html
5. Amiri Baraka, '*Jimmy!* – James Arthur Baldwin', *Eulogies* (New York: Marsilio Publishers, 1996), 96.
6. Gary Edward Holcomb, *Code Name Sasha: Queer Black Marxism and the Harlem Renaissance* (Gainesville: University Press of Florida, 2007), 12.

CHAPTER 1. TRANSNATIONAL BALDWIN

1. Cited by Magdalena Zaborowska, *James Baldwin's Turkish Decade: Erotics of Exile* (Durham and London: Duke University Press, 2009), 18.
2. James Baldwin, 'Smaller than Life', *The Nation* 165/3 (19 July 1947), 78.
3. Ibid, 78.

4. Geraldine Murphy, 'Subversive Anti-Stalinism: Race and Sexuality in the Early Essays of James Baldwin', *ELH* 63 (1996), 1034.
5. Rosa Bobia, *The Critical Reception of James Baldwin in France* (New York and Washington: Peter Lang, 1997), 13.
6. Unlike Baldwin's file, Richard Wright's is available on the FBI's website at www.fbi./gov/ The mention of Baldwin is in Wright's file, section 1b. There is no pagination but it is on p. 49.
7. See Baldwin's description of Wright's meeting of the Franco-American Fellowship Club in 'Alas, Poor Richard', *Collected Essays*, especially 264–5.
8. Isaacs, Harold, 'Five Writers and their Ancestors Part 2', *Phylon*, 21/4 (1960), 324.
9. Brent Hayes Edwards, *The Practice of Diaspora: Literature, Translation, and the Rise of Black Internationalism* (Cambridge, Mass. and London: Harvard University Press, 2003), 7.
10. Ibid, 5.
11. François Bondy, 'James Baldwin, as Interviewed by François Bondy', *Transition*, 0/12 (January–February 1964), 16.
12. In Baldwin's unpublished play, *The Welcome Table*, there is an assembled cast from different countries. See Leeming, *James Baldwin*, who reads the play as a work about 'exiles and alienation', 373–4.
13. Zaborowska notes in her discussion of Turkey that 'In cases when Baldwin brought up the issue of race himself, his nationality seemed to override his color in the eyes of his hosts. . . . He was noticed because he was black, but he was left alone because he was American' (87). Baldwin also explores the privilege of his American national status when he is imprisoned for the theft of a bed sheet in 'Equal in Paris'.
14. Zaborowska, *James Baldwin's Turkish Decade*, 110.
15. See Zaborowska's illuminating chapter on *The Welcome Table*, 249–64.
16. Zaborowska, *James Baldwin's Turkish Decade*, 17.
17. Ernest Champion, *Mr Baldwin, I Presume: James Baldwin – Chinua Achebe: A Meeting of Minds*. Foreword by David Leeming (New York and London: University Press of America, Inc., 1995), 86.

CHAPTER 2. THE WRITER AND THE CIVIL RIGHTS MOVEMENT

1. 'Nation: The Root of the Negro Problem', *Time* (17 May 1964), http://www.time.com/time/magazine/article/0,9171,830 326,00.html

2. Lynn Orilla Scott, 'Challenging the American Conscience, Re-Imagining the American Identity: James Baldwin and the Civil Rights Movement', in Douglas Field (ed.), *A Historical Guide to James Baldwin* (Oxford and New York: Oxford University Press, 2009), 146.
3. One exception is Lynn Scott's insightful overview of Baldwin's artistic and political contributions to the movement in my edited volume, *A Historical Guide to James Baldwin*.
4. The FBI files are paginated but are not strictly chronological. My page references refer to the FBI's pagination.
5. Natalie Robins, *Alien Ink: The FBI's War on the Freedom of Expression* (New Brunswick: Rutgers University Press, 1992), 228.
6. Harold Cruse, *The Crisis of the Negro Intellectual: A Historical Analysis of the Failure of Black Leadership* (1967; reprint with a foreword by Bazel E. Allen and Ernest J. Wilson III, New York: Quill, 1984), 194. Cruse also notes Norman Podhoretz's attempts to get Baldwin 'off that personal kick and make him talk about solutions and programs', which failed (194).
7. Eldridge Cleaver, *Soul on Ice* (New York and Toronto: Ramparts, 1968), 99, 102.
8. Ibid, 103.
9. Stanley Crouch, 'Meteor in a Black Hat', *Notes of a Hanging Judge: Essays and Reviews, 1979–1989* (New York and Oxford: Oxford University Press, 1990), 197; Amiri Baraka, *'Jimmy!* – James Arthur Baldwin', *Eulogies* (New York: Marsilio Publishers, 1996), 96.
10. Frantz Fanon, *Black Skins, White Masks*, trans. Charles Lam Markamm, introd. Homi K. Bhabha [1952] (London: Pluto Press, 1986), 170.
11. Eliot Fremont Smith, 'Books of the Times: Another Track', *New York Times* (31 May 1968), 27.

CHAPTER 3. RACIAL AND SEXUAL DIFFERENCE

1. Joseph Beam, 'Not A Bad Legacy Brother', in Essex Hemphill (ed.), *Brother to Brother: New Writings By Black Gay Men* (Boston: Alyson Publications, Inc., 1991), 185.
2. Andrea Lowenstein, 'James Baldwin and His Critics', *Gay Community News* (9 February 1980), 11.
3. Yasmin DeGout, 'Masculinity' and (Im)maturity: ''The Man Child'' and Other Stories in Baldwin's Gender Studies Enterprise', in D. Quentin Miller (ed.), *Re-Viewing James Baldwin: Things Not Seen* (Philadelphia: Temple University Press, 2000), 134.

4. Richard Goldstein, 'Go The Way Your Blood Beats: An Interview with James Baldwin', *Village Voice* 26 (June 1984), 13.
5. Ibid.
6. Ibid.
7. For an interesting comparison to Baldwin's comment, see James S. Tinney, 'Why A Black Gay Church?', in Joseph Beam (ed.), *In the Life: A Gay Black Anthology* (Boston: Alyson Publications, 1986) who asks, 'Is not religion, like sexuality, a personal thing between individuals and God?' (70).
8. *Tongues Untied*. Dir. Marlon Riggs (1989).
9. Jerome de Romanet, 'Revisiting *Madeleine* and "The Outing:" James Baldwin's Revisions of Gide's Sexual Politics', *Melus* 22/1 (spring 1997), 8.
10. Eldridge Cleaver, *Soul on Ice* (New York and Toronto: Ramparts, 1968), 110.
11. bell hooks, 'Reflections on Race and Sex', *Yearning: Race, Gender and Cultural Politics* (Boston: South End Press, 1990), 58.
12. Henry Louis Gates, Jr., 'The Welcome Table', in Gerald Early (ed.), *Lure and Loathing: Essays on Race, Identity and the Ambivalence of Assimilation* (London and New York: Allen Lane, 1993), 159.
13. Dwight McBride, 'Can the Queen Speak? Racial Essentialism, Sexuality and the Voice of Authority', *Callaloo* 21/2 (1998), 10.
14. See Samuel R. Delany and Joseph Beam, 'Samuel Delany: The Possibility of Possibilities', *In the Life: A Gay Black Anthology*, 185–208.
15. Ibid, 197, 196.
16. Emmanuel Nelson, 'The Novels of James Baldwin: Struggles of Self-Acceptance', *Journal of American Culture*, 8/4 (1985), 13. See also Carolyn Sylvander, *James Baldwin* (New York: Frederick Ungar Publishing, 1980), who notes that David is 'a negative and confusing embodiment of the homosexual experience' (51).
17. Donald Gibson, 'James Baldwin: The Political Anatomy of Space', in Therman B. O'Daniel (ed.), *James Baldwin: A Critical Evaluation* (Washington: Howard University Press, 1977), 9.
18. Gore Vidal, *The City and the Pillar*, reprint, with new preface by Vidal [1948] (London: Abacus, 1997), 65.
19. Fern Marja Eckman, *The Furious Passage of James Baldwin* (New York: M. Evans and Co, 1966), 32.
20. Ibid, 31.
21. Michael Cobb, *God Hates Fags: The Rhetorics of Religious Violence* (New York and London: New York University Press, 2006), 56.
22. See Eckman where Baldwin notes that he was nearly married three times, adding that his early years were struggles in coming to terms with what he would later call his bisexuality (112).

23. For a useful discussion of the term 'androgynous' in relation to Baldwin, see Kendall Thomas, '"Ain't Nothin' Like the Real Thing:" Black Masculinity, Gay Sexuality and the Jargon of Authenticity', in Marcellus Blount and George Cunningham (eds.), *Representing Black Men* (New York and London: Routledge, 1996), 56–61.

24. Susan Feldman, 'Reconciling Baldwin's Racial and Sexual Politics', *Re-Viewing James Baldwin: Things Not Seen*, 98.

25. William A. Cohen, 'Liberalism, Libido, Liberation: Baldwin's *Another Country*', in Patricia Juliana Smith (ed.), *The Queer Sixties* (New York and London: Routledge, 1999), 212.

26. Cohen, 'Liberalism, Libido, Liberation: Baldwin's *Another Country*', 212.

CHAPTER 4. BALDWIN AND MUSIC

1. James Baldwin, 'The Uses of the Blues', *Playboy* (January 1964), 131.

2. David Leeming, *James Baldwin: A Biography* (New York: Alfred A. Knopf, 1994), 206.

3. LeRoi Jones [Amiri Baraka], *Home: Social Essays* [1966] (New Jersey: The Ecco Press, 1998), 105–15.

4. Cited by Andrew Ross, *No Respect: Intellectuals and Popular Culture* (New York and London: Routledge, 1989), 68; see also Baldwin's *One Day When I Was Lost: A Scenario Based on the Autobiography of Malcolm X* (New York: Dell, 1972), where the screen directions refer to the sound of a 'white' jazz band (43, 82).

5. James Baldwin and Margaret Mead, *A Rap on Race* (New York: Dell, 1971), 70, 158.

6. James Lincoln Collier, 'Black Consciousness and the White Jazz Fan', in James Campbell (ed.), *The Picador Book of Blues and Jazz* (London: Picador, 1995), 332.

7. Baldwin, 'The Uses of the Blues', 132.

8. James Baldwin, 'Of the Sorrow Songs: The Cross of Redemption', *The Picador Book of Blues and Jazz*, 330.

9. Baldwin, 'The Uses of the Blues', 241.

10. Baldwin, 'Of the Sorrow Songs', 327.

11. Baldwin, 'The Uses of the Blues:' 131.

12. Baldwin, 'The Uses of the Blues', 241.

13. Cited by Rosa Bobia, *The Critical Reception of James Baldwin in France* (New York and Washington, Peter Lang, 1997), 37.

14. T. S. Eliot, *The Wasteland*, *The Complete Poems and Plays* (London: Faber and Faber, 1969), 62.

15. For an informative reading of Bessie Smith and Baldwin (with particular reference to *Another Country*), see Josh Kun, 'Life According to the Beat: James Baldwin, Bessie Smith and the Perilous Sounds of Love', *James Baldwin Now*, 307–28.
16. Baldwin also describes Ida listening to Billie Holiday recordings (159).
17. Baldwin, 'The Uses of the Blues', 241.
18. Zora Neale Hurston, 'The Sanctified Church and the Jook', *The Sanctified Church*, foreword by Toni Cade Bambara (New York: Marlow and Company, 1981), 136.
19. Baldwin, 'The Uses of the Blues', 131.
20. See Alan Young, *Woke Me Up This Morning: Black Gospel Singers and the Gospel Life* (University of Mississippi Press, 1997).
21. James Campbell, *Talking at the Gates: A Life of James Baldwin* (London and Boston: Faber and Faber, 1991), 281.
22. Ernest A. Champion, *Mr Baldwin, I Presume: James Baldwin – Chinua Achebe: A Meeting of Minds*, foreword by David Leeming (New York and London: University Press of America, Inc., 1995), 28, 100.
23. Cited by Lynn Orilla Scott, *James Baldwin's Later Fiction: Witness to the Journey* (Michigan: Michigan State University Press, 2002), 122.
24. Robert Reid-Pharr, *Once you Go Black: Choice, Desire, and the Black American Intellectual* (New York and London: New York University Press, 2007), 105.
25. Cited by Trudier Harris, 'The Eye as Weapon in *If Beale Street Could Talk*', in Fred Stanley and Nancy V. Burt (eds.), *Critical Essays on James Baldwin* (Boston: G. K. Hall and Co, 1988), 214. For a useful chapter on *If Beale Street*, see Harris's chapter, 'Bearing the Burden of the Blues: *If Beale Street Could Talk*', *Black Women in the Fiction of James Baldwin* (Knoxville: The University of Tennessee Press, 1985), 128–63.

CHAPTER 5. BALDWIN AND RELIGION

1. *James Baldwin: The Price of the Ticket*. Dir. Karen Thorsen, 1990.
2. James Campbell, *Talking at the Gates: A Life of James Baldwin* (London: Faber and Faber, 1991), 9, 10.
3. David Leeming, *James Baldwin: A Biography* (New York: Alfred A. Knopf, 1994). 23.
4. Ibid, 30.
5. Zora Neale Hurston, 'The Sanctified Church and the Jook', *The Sanctified Church*, foreword by Toni Cade Bambara (New York: Marlowe & Co., 1981), 103.

6. Langston Hughes, 'Tambourines to Glory', *Five Plays by Langston Hughes*, ed. and introd. Webster Smalley (Bloomington: Indiana University Press, 1968), 210.
7. Cheryl J. Sanders, *Saints in Exile: The Holiness-Pentecostal Experience in African-American Religion and Culture* (New York and Oxford: Oxford University Press, 1996), 4.
8. Cited by Barbara Olson, '"Come-to-Jesus Stuff" in James Baldwin's *Go Tell it on the Mountain* and *The Amen Corner'*, *African-American Review*, 31/2 (1997), 296.
9. James Cone, *Black Theology and Black Power* (New York: The Seabury Press, 1970), 72.
10. Leeming, *James Baldwin*, 89.
11. *Conversations with James Baldwin* (240) where Baldwin stated that *Go Tell it* was 'about my relationship to my father and to the church, which is the same thing really. It was an attempt to exorcise something . . .'
12. Harold Norse, *Memoirs of a Bastard Angel*, preface by James Baldwin (New York: William Morrow & Co., 1989), 114.
13. Cited by W. J. Weatherby, *James Baldwin: Artist on Fire* (London: Michael Joseph, 1990), 96. The original manuscript is more sexually explicit; see James Baldwin, typescript of *Go Tell it on the Mountain*. c. 1950 (The James Baldwin Collection. MG 278. The Schomburg Center for Research in Black Culture, New York Public Library).
14. Cited by Norse, *Memoirs of a Bastard Angel*, 114.
15. Bryan R. Washington, 'Wrestling with "The Love That Dare Not Speak Its Name": John, Elisha, and the "Master"', in Trudier Harris (ed.), *New Essays on Go Tell it on the Mountain* (Cambridge: Cambridge University Press, 1996) 78; see also Vivian M. May, 'Ambivalent Narratives, Fragmented Selves: Performative Identities and the Mutability of Roles in James Baldwin's *Go Tell it on the Mountain'*, in *New Essays on Go Tell it on the Mountain*, 97–126; cited by Fern Marja Eckman, *The Furious Passage of James Baldwin* (New York: M. Evans and Co, 1966), 30.
16. Michael Cobb, *God Hates Fags: The Rhetorics of Religious Violence* (New York and London: New York University Press, 2006), 53.
17. Ibid, 72.
18. Richard K. Barksdale, 'Temple of the Fire Baptized', in Fred L. Standley and Nancy V. Burt (eds.) *Critical Essays on James Baldwin* (Boston: G.K. Hall and Co., 1988), 145.
19. Clarence Hardy, *James Baldwin's God: Sex, Hope, and Crisis in Black Holiness Culture* (Knoxville: University of Tennessee Press, 2009), 26.

20. Cobb, *God Hates Fags*, 63.
21. John Hall 'James Baldwin: A Transition Interview', *Transition* 0/41 (1972), 24.
22. Cornel West, *Race Matters* (Boston: Beacon Press, 1993), 19; Martin Luther King, Jr., 'Love in Action', *Strength to Love* (London: Fontana Books, 1969), 50.
23. Cited by bell hooks, *Salvation: Black People and Love* (New York: Perennial, 2001), 7.

CONCLUSION

1. Carol E. Henderson, 'The Price of the Ticket: Baldwin Criticism in Perspective', in Douglas Field (ed.), *A Historical Guide to James Baldwin* (New York and Oxford: Oxford University Press, 2009), 246.
2. Toni Morrison, 'Life in His Language', *New York Times Book Review* (20 December 1987), 27.
3. Maya Angelou, 'A Brother's Love', *New York Times Book Review* (20 December 1987), 29.
4. Amiri Baraka, 'We Carry Him With Us', *New York Times Book Review* (20 December 1987): 27, 29.
5. John Wideman, 'Panel Discussion', in Jules Chametzky (ed.), *Black Writers Redefine Their Struggle: A Tribute to James Baldwin* (Massachusetts: University of Massachusetts Press, 1989), 66.
6. Emmanuel Nelson, 'Critical Deviance: Homophobia and the Reception of James Baldwin's Fiction', *Journal of American Culture* 14/3 (1991), 95.
7. Michael Thelwell, 'Panel Discussion', *Black Writers Redefine the Struggle*, 70.
8. Dwight A. McBride, 'Introduction: New Approaches to Baldwin', in McBride (ed.), *James Baldwin Now* (New York and London: New York University Press, 1999), 2.
9. See Arnold Rampersad's two volume biography of Langston Hughes, published by Oxford University Press in 1986/1988 and *Ralph Ellison: A Biography*, published by Knopf in 2007. The latter is 672 pages compared to Leeming's biography which weighs in at 442 pages. See also David Levering Lewis's Pulitzer prize winning biography of *W.E.B. Du Bois*. Originally published as two volumes in 1994/2001, it has been reissued by Henry Holt as one 912-page tome.

Select Bibliography

WORKS BY JAMES BALDWIN

Plays

Blues for Mister Charlie, 1964 (New York: Vintage, 1995).
The Amen Corner, 1968 (London: Penguin, 1991).

Novels

Go Tell it on the Mountain, 1953 (London: Penguin, 1991).
Giovanni's Room, 1956 (London: Penguin, 1990).
Another Country, 1962 (London: Penguin, 1990).
Tell Me How Long the Train's Been Gone, 1968 (London: Penguin, 1994).
If Beale Street Could Talk, 1974 (London: Penguin, 1974).
Just Above My Head, 1979 (London: Penguin, 1994).

Short Stories

Going to Meet the Man, 1965 (London: Penguin, 1991).
James Baldwin: Early Novels and Stories, ed. Toni Morrison (New York: Library of America, 1998).

Essays

Notes of a Native Son (Boston: Beacon Press, 1955).
Nobody Knows My Name: More Notes of a Native Son (New York: Dial Press, 1961).
The Fire Next Time (New York: Dial Press, 1963).
Nothing Personal, with photographs by Richard Avedon (New York: Atheneum, 1964).
No Name in the Street (New York: Dial Press, 1972).
The Devil Finds Work: An Essay (New York: Dial Press, 1976).

The Evidence of Things Not Seen (New York: Holt, Rinehart, & Winston, 1985).

The Price of the Ticket: Collected Nonfiction, 1948–1985 (New York: St Martin's Press/Marek, 1985).

James Baldwin: Collected Essays, ed. Toni Morrison (New York: Library of America 1998).

The Cross of Redemption: Uncollected Writings, ed. Randall Kenan (New York: Pantheon Books, 2010).

Poetry

Jimmy's Blues (New York: St Martin's Press, 1985); British edition published in 1983.

Gypsies and Other Poems. Edition limited to 325 copies (Leeds, Mass.: Gehenna Press/Eremite Press, 1989).

Screenplay

One Day When I Was Lost: A Scenario Based on Alex Haley's 'The Autobiography of Malcolm X' (London: Michael Joseph, 1972).

Children's Book

Little Man Little Man: A Story of Childhood. Illustrations by Yoran Cazac (New York: Dial Press, 1976).

Selected Interviews

Baldwin gave numerous interviews over the years, many of which remain uncollected. The following are collections, extended interviews or key uncollected interviews.

A Rap on Race: James Baldwin and Margaret Mead (Philadelphia: J. B. Lippincott, 1971).

A Dialogue: James Baldwin and Nikki Giovanni (Philadelphia: J. B. Lippincott, 1973).

Conversations with James Baldwin, eds. Fred Standley and Louis H. Pratt (Jackson: University Press of Mississippi, 1989).

Goldstein, Richard, 'Go the Way Your Blood Beats: An Interview with James Baldwin', in Quincy Troupe (ed.), *James Baldwin: The Legacy* (New York: Touchstone/Simon & Schuster, 1989), 173–85.

'Interview with Michael John Weber', in *Perspectives: Angels on African Art* (New York: Center for African Art, 1987), 113–27.

Isaacs, Harold, 'Five Writers and Their Ancestors Part 2', *Phylon*, 21/4 (1960), 317–336.

'James Baldwin, as Interviewed by François Bondy', *Transition*, 0/12 (January–February 1964), 12–19.

BIOGRAPHIES

Boyd, Herb, *Baldwin's Harlem: A Biography of James Baldwin* (New York: Atria Books, 2008).
Campbell, James, *Talking at the Gates: A Life of James Baldwin* (London: Faber and Faber, 1991).
Eckman, Fern Marja, *The Furious Passage of James Baldwin* (New York: M. Evans & Co, 1966).
Leeming, David A., *James Baldwin: A Biography* (New York: Knopf, 1994).
Weatherby, William J., *James Baldwin: Artist on Fire: A Portrait* (London: Michael Joseph, 1990).

CRITICAL STUDIES

Books on Baldwin

Balfour, Lawrie, *The Evidence of Things Not Said: James Baldwin and the Promise of American Democracy* (Ithaca, New York: Cornell University Press, 2001).
Bobia, Rosa, *The Critical Reception of James Baldwin in France* (New York: Peter Lang, 1997).
Champion, Ernest A., *Mr. Baldwin, I Presume: James Baldwin – Chinua Achebe, A Meeting of the Minds* (Landham, Md.: University Press of America, 1995).
Hardy, Clarence, *James Baldwin's God: Sex, Hope, and Crisis in Black Holiness Culture* (Knoxville: University of Tennessee Press, 2009).
Harris, Trudier, *Black Women in the Fiction of James Baldwin* (Knoxville: University of Tennessee Press, 1985).
Lee, Robert A., *James Baldwin: Climbing to the Light* (New York: St. Martin's Press, 1991).
Porter, Horace A., *Stealing the Fire: The Art and Protest of James Baldwin* (Middletown, Conn.: Wesleyan University Press, 1989).
Scott, Lynn Orilla, *Witness to the Journey: James Baldwin's Later Fiction* (East Lansing, Mich.: Michigan State University, 2002).
Sylvander, Carolyn Wedin, *James Baldwin* (New York: Ungar, 1980).
Zaborowska, Magdalena J., *James Baldwin's Turkish Decade: Erotics of Exile* (Duke University Press, 2009).

Collections of Essays

Chametzky, Jules (ed.), *Black Writers Redefine the Struggle: A Tribute to James Baldwin* (Amherst, Mass.: University of Massachusetts Press, 1989).

Field, Douglas (ed.), *A Historical Guide to James Baldwin* (New York and Oxford: Oxford University Press, 2009).

Harris, Trudier (ed.), *New Essays on Go Tell It on the Mountain* (Cambridge, England; New York: Cambridge University Press, 1996).

Henderson, Carol E. (ed.), *James Baldwin's Go Tell It on the Mountain: Historical and Critical Essays* (New York: Peter Lang, 2006).

King, Lovalerie and Lynn Orilla Scott (eds.), *James Baldwin and Toni Morrison: Comparative Critical and Theoretical Essays* (New York: Palgrave Macmillan, 2006).

Kollhofer, Jakob (ed.), *James Baldwin: His Place in American Literary History and His Reception in Europe* (Frankfurt am Main; New York: Peter Lang Publishers, 1991).

McBride, Dwight A. (ed.), *James Baldwin Now* (New York: New York University Press, 1999).

Miller, D. Quentin (ed.), *Re-Viewing James Baldwin: Things Not Seen* (Philadelphia: Temple University Press, 2000).

O'Daniel, Therman B. (ed.), *James Baldwin: A Critical Evaluation* (Washington, D.C.: Howard University Press, 1977).

Standley, Fred L. and Nancy V. Burt (eds.), *Critical Essays on James Baldwin* (Boston, Massachusetts: G. K. Hall and Company, 1988).

Troupe, Quincy (ed.), *James Baldwin: The Legacy* (New York: Simon and Schuster, 1989).

Parts of Books and Chapters in Books

Auger, Phillip, *Native Sons in No Man Land: Rewriting Afro-American Manhood in the Novels of Baldwin, Walker, Wideman, and Gaines* (New York: Garland Publishers, 2000).

Beam, Joseph, 'James Baldwin: Not a Bad Legacy, Brother' in Essex Hemphill (ed.), *Brother to Brother: New Writings By Black Gay Men* (Boston: Alyson Publications, Inc., 1991).

Butler, Cheryl B., 'James Baldwin: Voice of Prophecy' in *The Art of the Black Essay: From Meditation to Transcendence* (New York: Routledge, 2003).

Campbell, James, *Exiled in Paris: Richard Wright, James Baldwin, Samuel Beckett and Others on the Left Bank* (New York: Scribner, 1995).

Clark, Keith, *Black Manhood in James Baldwin, Ernest J. Gaines, and August Wilson* (Urbana: University of Illinois Press, 2002).

Cobb, Michael L., 'James Baldwin and His Queer, Religious Words' in *God Hates Fags: The Rhetorics of Religious Violence* (New York: New York University Press, 2006).

Cohen, William A., 'Liberalism, Libido, Liberation: Baldwin's *Another Country*' in Patricia Juliana Smith (ed.), *The Queer Sixties* (New York & London: Routledge, 1999).

Ezenwa-Ohaeto, 'Notions and Nuances: Africa in the Works of James Baldwin' in Femi Ojo-Ade (ed.), *Of Dreams Deferred, Dead or Alive: African Perspectives on African-American Writers* (London and Westport, Connecticut: Greenwood Press, 1996).

Field, Douglas, 'Passing as a Cold War Novel: Anxiety and Assimilation in James Baldwin's *Giovanni's Room*' in Field (ed.), *American Cold War Culture* (Edinburgh: Edinburgh University Press, 2005).

Gates, Henry Louis, Jr., 'The Welcome Table' in Gerald Early (ed.), *Lure and Loathing: Essays on Race, Identity and the Ambivalence of Assimilation* (London and New York: Allen Lane, 1993).

Gounard, Jean-François, *The Racial Problem in the Works of Richard Wright and James Baldwin* (Westport, Conn.: Greenwood Press, 1992).

Hakutani, Yoshinobu, 'No Name in the Street: James Baldwin's Exploration of American Urban Culture', in *Cross-Cultural Visions in African American Modernism: From Spatial Narrative to Jazz Haiku* (Columbus: Ohio State University Press, 2006).

——, 'If *Beale Street Could Talk*: Baldwin's Search for Love and Identity' in *Cross-Cultural Visions in African American Modernism: From Spatial Narrative to Jazz Haiku* (Columbus: Ohio State University Press, 2006).

Harris-Lopez, Trudier, 'Slanting the Truth: Homosexuality, Manhood, and Race in James Baldwin's *Giovanni's Room*', in *South of Tradition: Essays on African American Literature* (Athens: University of Georgia Press, 2002).

Henderson, Mae G., 'James Baldwin's *Giovanni's Room*: Expatriation, "Racial Drag", and Homosexual Panic', in E. Patrick Johnson and Mae G. Henderson (eds.), *Black Queer Studies: A Critical Anthology* (Durham, N.C.: Duke University Press, 2005).

Ikard, David, 'Black Patriarchy and the Dilemma of Black Women's Complicity in James Baldwin's *Go Tell It on the Mountain*' in *Breaking the Silence: Toward a Black Male Feminist Criticism* (Baton Rouge: Louisiana University Press, 2007).

Jimoh, A. Yemisi, 'Jazz Me Blues: Reading Music in James Baldwin's "Sonny's Blues"', in *Spiritual, Blues, and Jazz People in African American Fiction: Living in Paradox* (Knoxville: University of Tennessee Press, 2002).

103

Johnson-Roullier, Cyraina E., *Reading on the Edge: Exiles, Modernities, and Cultural Transformation in Proust, Joyce, and Baldwin* (Albany: State University of New York Press, 2000).

Margolies, Edward, 'Struggles for Space: Stephen Crane, James Baldwin, Ann Petry, Bernard Malamud', in *New York and the Literary Imagination: The City in Twentieth Century Fiction and Drama* (Jefferson, N.C.: McFarland and Company, 2008).

McBride, Dwight, 'Straight Black Studies: On African American Studies, James Baldwin, and Black Queer Studies', in E. Patrick Johnson and Mae G. Henderson (eds.), *Black Queer Studies: A Critical Anthology* (Durham, N.C.: Duke University Press, 2005).

Walker, Will, '*After the Fire Next Time*: James Baldwin's Post Consensus Double Bind', in Eddie S. Glaude, Jr. (ed.), *Is it Nation Time?: Contemporary Essays on Black Power and Black Nationalism* (Chicago: University of Chicago Press, 2002).

Wallace, Maurice O., 'On Being A Witness: Passion, Pedagogy, and the Legacy of James Baldwin', in E. Patrick Johnson and Mae G. Henderson (eds.), *Black Queer Studies: A Critical Anthology* (Durham, N.C.: Duke University Press, 2005).

Selected Articles and Reviews

Bell, Matt, 'Black Ground, Gay Figure: Working through *Another Country*, Black Power and Gay Liberation', *American Literature*, 79/3 (September 2007), 577–603.

Bigsby, C. W. E., 'The Divided Mind of James Baldwin', in Fred L. Standley and Nancy V. Burt (eds.), *Critical Essays on James Baldwin* (Boston: G. K. Hall & Co., 1988), 94–111.

Cedelstrom, Lorelei, 'Love, Race and Sex in the Novels of James Baldwin', *Mosaic*, 17/2 (Spring 1984), 175–188.

Corber, Robert J., 'Everybody Knew His Name: Reassessing James Baldwin', *Contemporary Literature*, 42/1 (Spring 2001), 166–75.

Davis, Nicholas K., 'Go Tell It on the Stage: *Blues for Mister Charlie* as Dialectical Drama', *Journal of American Drama and Theatre*, 17/2 (Spring 2005), 30–42.

Field, Douglas, 'Looking for Jimmy Baldwin: Sex, Piracy, and Black Nationalist Fervor', *Callaloo*, 27/2 (Spring 2004), 457–80.

Fielder, Leslie, 'Caliban or Hamlet: An American Paradox', *Encounter*, 26 (April 1966), 23–7.

Graves, Wallace, 'The Question of Moral Energy in James Baldwin's *Go Tell It on the Mountain*', *CLAJ* (March 1964), 215–23.

Jordan, June, 'If Beale Street Could Talk', *Village Voice* (20 June 1974), 33–5.

Lee, Susanna, 'The Jazz Harmonies of Connection and Disconnection in "Sonny's Blues"', *Genre*, 37/2 (Summer 2004), 285–300.

Lowenstein, Andrea, 'James Baldwin and His Critics', *Gay Community News* (9 February 1980), 10, 11, 17.

Lynch, Michael F., 'Beyond Guilt and Innocence: Redemptive Suffering in Baldwin's *Another Country*', *Obsidian* ii, 7/1 & 2 (Spring-Summer 1992), 1–18.

Miller, Elise, 'The "Maw of Western Culture": James Baldwin and the Anxieties of Influence', *African American Review*, 38/4 (Winter 2004), 625–36.

Moon, Sahng Young, 'African Americans and Colonialism: James Baldwin's Essays in the Era of the Civil Rights Movement', *Journal of English Language and Literature*, 47/4 (Winter 2001), 941–57.

Murphy, Geraldine, 'Subversive Anti-Stalinism: Race and Sexuality in the Early Essays of James Baldwin', *ELH*, 63 (1996), 1021–46.

Nelson, Emmanuel, 'Critical Deviance: Homophobia and the Reception of James Baldwin's Fiction', *Journal of American Culture*, 14 (1991), 91–6.

Norman, Brian, 'James Baldwin's Confrontation with U.S. Imperialism in *If Beale Street Could Talk*', *MELUS*, 32/1 (Spring 2007), 119–38.

Nowlin, Michael, 'Ralph Ellison, James Baldwin, and the Liberal Imagination', *Arizona Quarterly*, 60/2 (Summer 2004), 117–40.

Ohi, Kevin, '"I'm Not the Boy You Want": Sexuality, "Race", and Thwarted Revelation in Baldwin's *Another Country*', *African American Review*, 33/2 (Summer 1999), 261–81.

Powers, Kerry, 'The Treacherous Body: Isolation, Confession, and Community in James Baldwin', *American Literature*, 77/4 (December 2005), 787–813.

Redding, J. Saunders, 'Since Richard Wright', *African Forum*, 1 (Spring 1966), 21–3.

Reid, Robert, 'The Powers of Darkness in "Sonny's Blues"', *CLA*, 43/4 (June 2000), 443–53.

Robinson, Angelo R., 'The Other Proclamation in James Baldwin's *Go Tell It on the Mountain*', *CLA*, 48/3 (March 2005), 336–51.

Ryan, Katy, 'Falling in Public: Larsen's *Passing*, McCarthy's *The Group*, and Baldwin's *Another Country*', *Studies in the Novel*, 36/1 (Spring 2004), 95–119.

Tackach, James, 'The Biblical Foundation of James Baldwin's "Sonny's Blues"', *Renascence: Essays on Values in Literature*, 59/2 (Winter 2007), 109–18.

Tóibín, Colm, 'The Last Witness', *London Review of Books*, 23/18 (20 September 2001), 15–20.

Wright, David, 'No Hiding Place: Exile "Underground" in James Baldwin's "This Morning, This Evening, So Soon"', *CLA*, 42/4 (June 1999), 445–61.

Films and Documentaries on James Baldwin

Biography: James Baldwin: Witness. Written and directed by Angie Corcetti and Helen Hood Scheer. Peter Jones Production Inc., 20 February 2003.

Go Tell it on the Mountain. Directed by Stan Lathan. California: Monterey Video, 1985. Reissued on DVD 3 February 2004.

I Heard it Through the Grapevine. Directed by Dick Fontaine and Pat Hartley. Living Archives, Inc., 1982.

James Baldwin. Produced by Jerry Baber and Amy A. Tiehel. Directed by Amy A. Tiehel. Bela Cynwyd, PA: Schlessinger Video Production, 1994.

James Baldwin: From Another Place. Directed by Sedat Pakay (1973).

James Baldwin: Patience and Shuffle the Cards. Written and directed by James Baldwin. Reissued by Benchmark Media, 1998.

James Baldwin: Price of the Ticket. Directed by Karen Thorsen. A Nobody Knows Production, Maysles Film. San Francisco: California Newsreel, 1989.

Pressure/Baldwin's Nigger. Directed by Horace Ové. Bfi Video, 1969. Reissued on DVD 26 September 2005.

106

Index

Lightning Source UK Ltd.
Milton Keynes UK
UKOW051932141211

183772UK00001B/4/P